GOVERNMENT PROCEDURES AND OPERATIONS

ASSESSING IMPEDIMENTS OF JOB CREATION

Government Procedures and Operations

Additional books in this series can be found on Nova's website under the Series tab.

Additional E-books in this series can be found on Nova's website under the E-book tab.

Economic Issues, Problems and Perspectives

Additional books in this series can be found on Nova's website under the Series tab.

Additional E-books in this series can be found on Nova's website under the E-book tab.

GOVERNMENT PROCEDURES AND OPERATIONS

ASSESSING IMPEDIMENTS OF JOB CREATION

JOSHUA A. LANCOLM
EDITOR

Nova Science Publishers, Inc.
New York

For permission to use material from this book please contact us:
Telephone 631-231-7269; Fax 631-231-8175
Web Site: http://www.novapublishers.com

Library of Congress Cataloging-in-Publication Data

Assessing impediments of job creation / editor, Joshua A. Lancolm.
p. cm.
Includes index.
ISBN 978-1-61324-352-7 (hbk.)
1. Job creation--United States. 2. Manpower policy--United States. 3. Labor policy--United States. 4. Unemployment--United States. I. Lancolm, Joshua A.
HD5724.A76 2011
331.12'04240973--dc22 2011011464

Published by Nova Science Publishers, Inc. † New York

CONTENTS

PREFACE

Over the past decade, global health has become a priority in U.S. foreign policy, and U.S. funding for related efforts has more than tripled. Neglected tropical diseases (NTDs), an important focus of U.S. global health assistance, may come under scrutiny as the 112th Congress debates spending levels for ongoing global health programs. Estimates indicate that some 2 billion people are at risk of contracting an NTD, of whom more than 1 billion people are afflicted with one or more. This book examines the background, responses and issues for Congress relating to Neglected Tropical Diseases (NTDs), while identifying research gaps and opportunities.

Chapter 1-Historically high unemployment rates remain a grave concern for American households. According to the Bureau of Labor Statistics (BLS), the unemployment rate for February 2011 was an unacceptably high 9 percent.[1] Unfortunately, the lower rate (down from 9.4 percent) may be due in part to individuals who have simply given up looking for work because their unemployment benefits have run out; thus, no longer meeting the government's official definition of "unemployed."[2]

Chapter 2- Testimony of Jay Timmons, President and CEO of National Association of Manufacturers, given before the Committee on Oversight and Government Reform during the Hearing on Regulatory Impediments to Job Creation.

Chapter 3- Testimony of Harry C. Alford, on behalf of the National Black Chamber of Commerce (NBCC), given before the Committee on Oversight and Government Reform during the Hearing on Regulatory Impediments to Job Creation.

Chapter 4- Testimony of Tom Nassif, President and CEO of Western Growers, given before the Committee on Oversight and Government Reform during the Hearing on Regulatory Impediments to Job Creation.

Chapter 5- Testimony of Michael J. Fredrich, President of MCM Composites, LLC., given before the Committee on Oversight and Government Reform during the Hearing on Regulatory Impediments to Job Creation.

Chapter 6- Testimony of Jack Buschur, President of Buschur Electric, given before the Committee on Oversight and Government Reform during the Hearing on Regulatory Impediments to Job Creation.

Chapter 7- Testimony of James Gattuso, Senior Research Fellow in Regulatory Policy of The Heritage Foundation, given before the Committee on Oversight and Government Reform during the Hearing on Regulatory Impediments to Job Creation.

Chapter 8- Testimony of Karen Kerrigan, President and CEO of Small Business and Entrepreneurship Council, given before the Committee on Oversight and Government Reform during the Hearing on Regulatory Impediments to Job Creation.

Assessing Impediments of Job Creation
Editor: Joshua A. Lancolm
ISBN: 978-1-61324-352-7

Chapter 1

ASSESSING REGULATORY IMPEDIMENTS TO JOB CREATION*

United States House of Representatives

U.S. House of Representatives
Committee on Oversight and Government Reform
Darrell Issa (CA-49), Chairman

Assessing Regulatory Impediments to Job Creation
PRELIMINARY STAFF REPORT
U.S. HOUSE OF REPRESENTATIVES
112TH CONGRESS
FEBRUARY 9, 2011

FINDINGS

- Jobs lost in construction, manufacturing, and administrative and support services represent almost 2/3 of the total jobs lost since May 2008. These hardest hit industries have seen little improvement in employment rates since the beginning of the recession.

---

* This is an edited, reformatted and augmented version of the United States House of Representatives Committee on Oversight and Government Reform Preliminary Staff Report, dated February 9, 2011.

- Small businesses are the engines that propel the American economy forward – they provide half of all private sector jobs and they represent 99.7 percent of all employer firms – totaling over 27 million businesses in this country. However, according to a recent survey, only four percent of small businesses indicate that they plan to create new jobs in the next few months.
- As important as small businesses are to the growth and prosperity of the American economy, they are also the most sensitive to the burden imposed by federal regulations. According to one study, small firms bear a regulatory cost of $10,585 per employee whereas large firms with more than 500 employees incur a cost of $7,755 per employee to comply with Federal regulations.
- The proprietor of a small business typically serves as the regulatory enforcer within her company – a role that is difficult to perform when so many other tasks need to be fulfilled, and when regulations are crafted that fail to take this challenging situation into account.
- Manufacturing is the industry hit the hardest by regulatory costs, with per firm costs at $688,944 – half a million dollars greater than the national average cost for all industries.
- Small manufacturers bear a proportionally larger regulatory burden with an estimated cost of $26,316 per employee – more than double the burden that is faced by larger manufacturers.
- The significant regulatory burden on American manufacturers complicates their ability to compete with international trade partners. According to research commissioned by the National Association of Manufacturers, "structural costs imposed on U.S. manufacturers including regulation create a 17.6 percent cost disadvantage when compared with nine major industrialized countries."
- Uncertainty of future regulation chills capital formation and can leave U.S. businesses with less investment capital if the money is diverted to foreign markets.
- Environmental Protection Agency (EPA) revocation of a longstanding and legitimate permit to operate at the Spruce No. 1 coal mine in Logan County, West Virginia provides a prime example of government action that job creators say creates significant uncertainty and exerts a chilling effect on future investment.
- As regulators in the United States may be creating unnecessary regulatory uncertainty, our international competitors are seeking to

entice America's potential job creators to set up shop within their borders - taking steps to make their countries more attractive to foreign investors.

- In many cases the benefits to society of a new regulation can outweigh these costs. For example, government-required nutrition labels on food products provide consumers with important information about the products they consume in a uniform format.
- EPA's handling of the Boiler Heater Maximum Achievable Control Technology (Boiler MACT), is an example of the Agency getting the cost benefit balance wrong. By the agency's own admission, the proposed rule was too aggressive and was not informed by adequate information about the affected industries. However, due to a court order, and EPA's initial aggressive approach to implementation, EPA will be forced to issue Boiler MACT by February 20, 2011.
- The debate over the impact of federal regulation lies not in whether an agency should regulate, rather with how the agency exercises the discretion that Congress has granted to it.
- The administrative process to develop rules and regulations should be executed with maximum transparency and predictability, while also providing the regulated community with a meaningful opportunity for dialogue with those crafting the regulatory mandates.
- On January 21, 2011, President Obama issued E.O. 13563 directing agencies to "take into account...the cost of cumulative regulations." This directive is an important step towards understanding how the Federal government should work with the private sector. Job creators do not live in a world where they are only subject to one regulation issued by one agency. Rather, job creators are subject to a myriad of regulations and compliance obligations.
- The utilities sector offers fertile ground to begin to understand how federal agencies should take into account the cumulative impact of regulations: from early 2009 to 2017, the industry will have to contend with no less than 35 separate regulatory deadlines. Those affected say looming regulatory changes have already caused two power plants to shut down early.
- While the Department of Labor has pulled back on two of its most controversial proposals, OSHA noise standards and OSHA Form 300 Musculoskeletal Disorders (MSD) reporting requirements; job creators expressed significant concern for the OSHA Combustible

Dust Management rule, proposed changes in OSHA Consultation Agreements, and OSHA's Injury & Illness Prevention Program ("I2P2").

- There is some evidence that regulations affecting the financial services industry may limit the job creation and growth capabilities of U.S., reducing economic growth by as much as 4 percent. The Dodd-Frank Wall Street Reform and Consumer Protection Act requires the issuance of nearly 500 rulemakings from a number of federal agencies.
- Respondents identified over 60 regulatory actions taken by the Environmental Protection Agency that could have a negative impact on job creation. Almost half the respondents identified the following three rules as job killing regulations: Boiler MACT, GHG regulations, and NAAQS for Ozone.

I. INTRODUCTION

Historically high unemployment rates remain a grave concern for American households. According to the Bureau of Labor Statistics (BLS), the unemployment rate for February 2011 was an unacceptably high 9 percent.[1] Unfortunately, the lower rate (down from 9.4 percent) may be due in part to individuals who have simply given up looking for work because their unemployment benefits have run out; thus, no longer meeting the government's official definition of "unemployed."[2]

The Administration's economic strategies employed over the last two years have not succeeded in getting Americans back to work in sufficient numbers. Against the backdrop, President Barack Obama has opened the door to determining whether government actions are hampering private sector job creation. In his State of the Union Address he called for a government-wide examination of regulations, to "help our companies compete" and to "knock down barriers that stand in the way of their success." The President has reached out to several organizations representing business interests in the preceding weeks and months and has invited the heads of some of the largest national and multinational companies to share their suggestions for jumpstarting the economy. Businesses that responded to the President overwhelmingly reported that regulations are the barriers to pushing the economy forward and creating much-needed jobs to boost recovery.[3]

Recognizing the need to create jobs and get Americans back to work, the House Oversight and Government Reform Committee is uniquely positioned to conduct a broad-based, economy-wide examination of the barriers that stand in the way of job growth and economic recovery. While still the Ranking Member, Congressman Issa focused on regulatory excess as a major barrier to job creation. Accordingly, he began reaching out to over 150 businesses, trade associations, and think tanks in December of 2010 to gauge the regulated community's concerns about regulations that affect their ability to create jobs.

On January 18, 2011, President Obama singled out regulatory barriers as a major obstacle to job creation and issued a Presidential Executive Order and accompanying Memoranda, signaling his concern about regulatory excess. Chairman Issa pledged to share the results of his study and analysis with the President and the American people, so that Congress and the Executive Branch can work together to minimize needless regulatory costs that create roadblocks for economic growth and private sector job creation. Some of the regulations identified by respondents were recently withdrawn, such as OSHA's proposed interpretation on occupational noise, or postponed, such as EPA's reconsideration of National Ambient Air Quality Standards (NAAQS) for Ozone. However, many regulations that appear to impose a large burden on the private sector, while providing a dubious benefit to the public, still remain on course and on the books.

This preliminary staff report and subsequent hearings will undertake a detailed, cross-jurisdictional look at the industries that have been hardest hit by the recession, with an emphasis on understanding their challenges and identifying rules cited as costly and problematic. Particular attention will be paid to rules that have not followed standard process and procedure – possibly violating Due Process protections for the regulated community, in addition to imposing high costs.

II. The Economy – Who is Hurting?

Despite the pronouncement of the end of the 2007-2009 recession, the unemployment rate has improved very little and remains historically and unacceptably high. In January 2011, the total number of unemployed persons in the United States was 13.9 million.[4] Absent a major change in policy, forecasts predict unemployment levels will remain at unacceptable levels through 2011.

While the unemployment figures are stunning, other indicators further explain the seriousness of the current unemployment situation. The most recent recession saw the sharpest increase in the unemployment rate of any post-World War II recession, with an overall increase of 4.5 percent as of 2009.[5] The number of jobless who have been unemployed for 52 weeks or longer has reached the staggering number of 4.5 million – nearly 31 percent of the total number of unemployed. In 2007, 9.5 percent of the unemployed had been unemployed for this amount of time.[6] Furthermore, the unemployment rate has remained above nine percent for 21 consecutive months, the longest stretch at such a high level since World War II.[7] Some Americans have been unemployed for longer and with less hope of finding work than at any point in the last 70 years.

Furthermore, the current unemployment crisis continues to affect minority groups disproportionately. According to December 2010 data, 13 percent of Latinos were unemployed, as were 15.8 percent of blacks, whereas 8.5 percent of whites were jobless.[8] More than half of black males between the ages of 16 and 19 are unemployed, and that's only counting those seeking work. Economists say legions of other young black men — nobody knows how many — have given up looking.[9]

Non-college graduates have also been disproportionately affected as the most recent unemployment rate for those with at least a high school diploma, 9.8 percent, and for those without, 15.3 percent, are double and triple the rates of the most educated, 4.8 percent.[10] These figures show that unemployment continues to have a disparate impact on minorities, as well as the less educated, and those groups continue to bear the largest burden of jobless woes.

Sustained levels of high unemployment have led to widespread negative public opinion of the American economy. Job security and unemployment are on the minds of nearly every American as 2011 begins with unemployment rates nearly double the historical average of five percent.[11] A January 2011 Gallup poll stated that 29 percent of Americans believe unemployment is the "No.1 problem facing the United States at the start of 2011."[12] Further, the prolonged economic morass helps explain why, in a recent survey, 87 percent listed the economy as a very important issue for the new Congress to tackle.[13]

A. Unemployment Rates Across the Country

Unemployment rates among the states have varied. California, Nevada, Oregon, Michigan, Florida, Georgia, South Carolina, and Rhode Island currently have unemployment rates over 10 percent.[14] Nevada continues to have the highest rate of unemployment in the country at 14.3 percent, followed by California and Michigan, each with unemployment at 12.4 percent, and Florida, with 12 percent of residents looking for work.[15] However, the Washington, D.C.-Arlington-Alexandria region had the lowest jobless rate in any metropolitan area in the country for November 2010, at 6 percent.

B. Painfully High Unemployment Rates in Certain Industries

Just as unemployment has adversely affected some regions in the United States more than others, certain industries have seen greater increases in unemployment levels than others. Jobs lost in construction, manufacturing, and administrative and support services represent almost two-thirds of the total jobs lost since May 2008.[16] In addition, the trucking industry was hit very hard through 2010 as a decrease in consumption and production, and an increase in fuel prices, forced companies to cut jobs from a usually robust industry.[17]

The hardest hit industries have seen little improvement in employment rates since the beginning of the recession. For example, employment in construction and manufacturing industries continued to trend flat throughout most of 2010.[18] Moreover, the BLS projections through 2018 speculate that the number of manufacturing jobs will actually decrease within the manufacturing industry, translating to a net loss in employment opportunities in this sector. [19] In these two industries BLS projects that nearly 1.4 million jobs will be lost by 2018 even without accounting for a continued recession. This projected loss underscores the continuing downward trend in goods-producing employment.[20]

Along with the construction and manufacturing sectors, other industries began to experience increased job losses in 2010. The retail industry, largely comprised of small businesses, experienced losses in November in the department store and furniture and home furnishing store sectors.[21] Monthly job losses in financial activities averaged 29,000 in 2009, but have since decelerated to 8,000 per month in 2010.[22]

To date, government workers have the lowest unemployment rate of any industry or class of worker in the nation at only 4.4 percent.[23] Moreover, the size of the federal government also expanded during the recession. While the private sector lost 7.2 million jobs since January 2008, the federal government gained 98,000 jobs – an increase of 3.5 percent of its work force.[24]

C. Small Business Impact

The downturn in the economy has taken its toll on small businesses over the past three years. Recent employment numbers show that only nine percent of small businesses report unfilled job openings in November 2010, the indicator that the industry uses to determine job expansion.[25] A low percentage of job openings mean that small businesses are not expanding; hence, there are few vacant positions that need to be filled. Of these small businesses, only four percent indicate that they plan to create new jobs in the next few months.[26] As small business is the lifeblood of the American economy, these numbers show how stymied the employment recovery has become. While small businesses saw slight economic improvements at the end of 2010, many indicators remain at recession levels, and reports show that these businesses have not yet entered recovery mode.[27]

III. Turning the Economy Around – Focus on Regulatory Barriers

Economic policies advanced over the last two years have failed to get Americans back to work. It is essential to go a step further and determine whether government actions are hampering private sector job creation. If government is standing in the way, it is also imperative to identify which policies are causing problems for which parts of the private sector and to take corrective action.

In response to an inquiry from then OMB Director Peter R. Orszag, the Business Roundtable informed the White House that "[m]any regulations and legislation – both existing and proposed – exacerbate the uncertainty created by today's volatile economic environment. Virtually every new regulation has an impact on recovery, competitiveness, and job creation. Often that impact is negative."[28] Regulations are on the mind of business leaders as they make strategic investment decisions and plan for future job growth.

President Obama has also been advised by his Economic Advisory Panel - which includes chief executives from GE, Caterpillar, and UBS - that regulations are harming businesses. This panel suggested measures that could be implemented in order to quell the expansion of such rules.[29] After the meeting, President Obama remarked that "what we are trying to do is go through very systematically to see where we can eliminate unnecessary red tape, unnecessary bureaucracy, regulations that have outlived their usefulness." The President has continued to meet with CEOs of major corporations; in December of 2010 he met with Mike Duke of Wal-Mart,[30] and hosted a CEO summit with 20 executives from Google, Cisco, IBM, American Express, DOW Chemical, and PepsiCo.[31] The theme of these meetings were similar; as the Administration explained, they were to take "...a balanced approach to regulation that will promote, rather than undermine, economic growth."[32]

The Obama Administration has done a significant amount of outreach to some of the largest national and multinational companies in order to learn about the concerns of the private sector. However, this strategy risks leaving out the millions of small business owners and businesses that have been affected by the recession at even greater levels. An inclusive outreach effort, that takes into consideration this important part of the American economy, is necessary to determine how regulations affect the smallest of businesses.

This report identifies the regulations that may be hindering job growth with particular focus on the concerns of small businesses.

A. Importance of Small Business in the American Economy

Small businesses are the engines that propel the American economy forward. President Barack Obama has accurately stated:

> ...[S]mall businesses produce most of the new jobs in this country. They are the anchors of our Main Streets. They are part of the promise of America –
>
> the idea that if you've got a dream and you're willing to work hard, you can succeed. That's what leads a worker to leave a job to become her own boss. That's what propels a basement inventor to sell a new product – or an amateur chef to open a restaurant. It's this promise that has drawn millions to our shores and made our economy the envy of the world.[33]

In fact, small businesses employ half of all private sector workers and they represent 99.7 percent of all employer firms – totaling over 27 million businesses in this country.[34] In addition, they are responsible for more than half of the nonfarm private GDP, and in recent years provided for 64 percent of newly created jobs.[35] These businesses are also significant contributors to research and development and technological innovation.[36] The growth and sustainability of small businesses are critical to the success of the American economy and, as the President alluded, maintaining the promise of the American dream.

However, as important as small businesses are to the growth and prosperity of the American economy, they are also the most sensitive to the burden imposed by federal regulations. In 2008, the cost of U.S. federal government regulations was an estimated $1.75 trillion.[37] The average cost burden on U.S. firms of any size was approximately $161,000,[38] not accounting for any costs extended onwards to consumers.[39] This amount exceeds the average firm's contributions to the payroll tax for Social Security and Medicaid.[40] Since many of the costs associated with regulations are "fixed," small firms, those that have less than 20 employees, disproportionately bear the costs of regulation.

These small firms are not able to distribute the costs over large amounts of revenue or output as bigger firms are able to do.[41] Further illustrating this point, small firms bear a regulatory cost of $10,585 per employee whereas regulatory costs for those firms with greater than 500 employees are $7,755 per employee.[42] Since 89 percent of firms in the United States employ fewer than 20 employees, the smallest businesses are shouldering a disproportionate regulatory burden.[43]

According to Philip Brady, President of the National Automobile Dealers Association (NADA), "regulations impose a shadow cost structure that presents an ongoing impediment to the nation's economic vitality."[44] NADA is a trade association that represents 17,000 new car and truck dealers, many of which are small businesses, employing about one million employees nationwide. Each year, NADA compiles an updated list of regulations that affect its member companies. This document, entitled "The Regulatory Maze," presents an extensive list that describes the massive number of regulations with which automobile businesses must comply on an annual basis.[45] The latest report reveals that 20 federal departments and agencies and 150 rules currently regulate a typical dealership operation.[46]

B. Small Manufacturers Hit the Hardest by Regulation

As Congress seeks to understand the policies that are holding back America's job creators, it is also important to observe the disparity in regulatory impact among small firms in specific industries in America. Studies show that, for firms of all sizes, manufacturing is the industry hit the hardest by regulatory costs, with per firm costs at $688,944 – half a million dollars greater than the national average cost for all industries.[47] Moreover, manufacturing firms that have 20 or fewer employees bear the greatest burden of any job creators in America, with an estimated cost of $26,316 per employee – this is more than double the burden that is faced by larger manufacturers.[48] This heavy weight is made harder to bear when one considers the lesser regulatory costs imposed on major foreign competitors - U.S. manufacturers have 17.6 percent higher baseline costs due to domestic regulations as compared to manufacturers in other countries.[49]

Small manufacturers operate and employ workers throughout the country. Employment data shows that ten states rely on manufacturing for ten percent or more of their total employment as of October 2010: Alabama, Connecticut, Indiana, Michigan, Minnesota, North Carolina, Ohio, South Carolina, Tennessee, and Wisconsin.[50] In addition, another seven states count manufacturing as at least eight percent of total employment: California, Georgia, Illinois, Missouri, Pennsylvania, Texas, and Washington. Given this data, regulatory costs affecting manufacturing have a significant impact on many states throughout the country. Note that California, Georgia, and Michigan lead the nation in terms of high unemployment rates, as well as dependence on small manufacturers as a source of job creation. Policies that hurt small manufacturers will have serious ramifications for the unemployed in these states.

C. Regulatory Uncertainty Exacerbates the Negative Impact of too Onerous Regulations

Regulators can create unnecessary uncertainty for businesses attempting to make strategic decisions, delaying and discouraging investment. Uncertainty of future regulation chills capital formation and can leave U.S. businesses with less investment capital if the money is diverted to foreign markets.[51] Financial experts have spoken out about this. For example, Richard Fisher, President of the Federal Reserve Bank of Dallas, stated that "[b]usinesses and consumers are being confronted with so many potential changes in the taxes and regulations that govern their behavior that they are uncertain about how to proceed downfield."[52] He also said that entrepreneurs are waiting for clearer signals from the nation's fiscal authorities and regulators before they act.[53] Reinforcing this sentiment, Tom Tauke, Executive Vice President for Verizon, stated that "a stable tax policy and eliminating regulatory uncertainty are . . . pivotal to attracting investment."[54]

The recent decision by the Environmental Protection Agency (EPA) to revoke a longstanding and legitimate permit to operate at the Spruce No. 1 coal mine in Logan County, West Virginia provides a prime example of government action that creates significant uncertainty and exerts a chilling effect on future investment.[55] According to West Virginia Senator Joe Manchin, "[t]his is not just an assault on the coal industry. It's an assault on every job market in the U.S. economy. It might be West Virginia and the coal industry today. It will be your industry tomorrow."[56]

D. Uncertainty at Home Makes Relocation Abroad More Attractive

As regulators in the United States may be creating unnecessary regulatory uncertainty, other countries are seeking to entice America's potential job creators to set up shop within their borders. Our competitors are aware of the important role that regulations have on investment and are taking steps to make their countries more attractive to foreign investors. For example, the European Commission (EC) adopted a policy of establishing impact assessments of regulations that will affect businesses.

These assessments take into consideration how the regulations will affect competitiveness for European firms.[57] The EC has also established Business Test Panels that collect information from businesses to assist in the regulatory cost analysis.[58]

Just as international competition exists for the most hospitable regulatory environment, this same competition exists between states. For example, in California, the constant flux of the regulatory state was cited as a major reason that businesses could not effectively do long-term planning, forcing them to leave the state, taking jobs and tax revenue elsewhere.[59] A July 2010 report issued by the Milken Institute attributes the departure of 79,000 manufacturing jobs from California between 2003 and 2007 to onerous regulations and high taxes.[60] The state experience can serve as a lesson to the federal government, as it is essentially a microcosm of the international competition between the United States and foreign countries. On the whole, the uncertainty of the American regulatory system puts the U.S. at a competitive disadvantage with the European Union and many other nations.

E. Poor Allocation of Scarce Resources

A common misconception is that new regulatory requirements can translate into new compliance positions, which should help put people back to work. However, regulatory compliance burdens actually divert resources away from productive positions and channel investment toward compliance roles. Economists refer to a misallocation of resources "when capital and labor are directed to less productive or unproductive uses."[61] Resources and personnel devoted to regulatory compliance are not able to contribute towards producing the goods and services that consumers value.

However necessary the compliance positions may be, they do not contribute to the bottom line of businesses because they are not part of the production cycle. This diversion of labor and capital effectively increases costs, reduces competitiveness, and hence discourages job creation. Therefore, regulations requiring the hiring of additional compliance staff, drain resources away from positions that could help businesses grow.

Accordingly, assessing regulatory impact on job growth should also focus on the types of jobs that are lost or created and how those jobs can benefit economic growth.[62]

An example of government mandated diversion of resources comes from the construction industry, which has experienced excessively high unemployment rates from the recession, reaching almost 20 percent - double the national rate.[63] Because of the depressed construction market, an owner of a construction firm reduced the size of his staff from 136 employees to just 66.[64] The additional burden associated with the expanded Form 1099 filing requirements flowing from the Patient Protection and Affordable Care Act will force him to hire an additional full-time employee to work in the accounting department.[65] However, this compliance position will not contribute to the company's productivity, will not create goods or services that can be sold, and, therefore, will not help the company grow and invest in additional jobs. The cost of compliance staff is simply a burden to be born.

IV. The Role of Congress and the Oversight and Government Reform Committee

While it is an undeniable fact that regulations impose a cost on the economy, it is similarly true that in some cases benefits from regulation to society can outweigh these costs. For example, government-required nutrition labels on food products provide consumers with important information about the products they consume in a uniform format. The debate over the affect of federal regulation lies not in whether an agency should regulate, but rather with how the agency exercises the discretion granted by Congress. The deliberative process should be executed with maximum transparency and predictability, while also providing the regulated community with a meaningful opportunity for dialogue with those crafting the regulatory mandates. With these goals in mind, Congress has passed several statutes to govern the regulatory process, so that the costs to the regulated community are minimized to the greatest extent possible when regulations are implemented.

Statutes that govern the regulatory process that are within the legislative jurisdiction of the Committee include the Paperwork Reduction Act, the Unfunded Mandates Reform Act, and the Data Quality Act. The Paperwork Reduction Act (PRA) created the Office of Information and Regulatory Affairs (OIRA) in 1980 as an office within OMB. The goal of the PRA was to streamline the clearinghouse process and, as its name implies, reduce the amount of government paperwork. Under the PRA, OIRA's responsibilities include "information policy, information collection request, clearance, and paperwork control, statistical policy and coordination, records management, privacy, and automatic data processing and telecommunications."[66]

Shortly after OIRA's creation, President Reagan augmented the role of the agency with Executive Order 12291 on "Federal Regulation."[67] The Executive Order required Cabinet departments to consider regulatory action only if the "benefits to society outweighed the costs," to prepare a "regulatory impact analysis" for any regulation with an annual economic impact of $100 million, and to require each agency to send OMB proposed and final rules for review.[68] The OMB review component was then given to OIRA through the responsibilities enumerated in the PRA.[69] President Reagan further enhanced OIRA's role through Executive Order 12498.[70] Under this Order, OIRA could return draft rules to agencies if there was no advance notice of the rule.[71] This process allowed OIRA to become aware of agency rulemaking before it occurred and thereby implement regulatory changes before rulemaking could be submitted in draft form.[72]

President George H.W. Bush continued the Reagan Executive Orders during his administration.

In 1993, President Bill Clinton revoked the Reagan-era Executive Orders and replaced them with executive order 12866.[73] This Executive Order recognized that regulatory policies could place unreasonable costs on the private sector, the "best engines for economic growth."[74] Agencies were required to tailor regulations to be less burdensome on society, to implement cost-benefit analysis for significant regulations (those with economic impacts of $100 million or more) and to submit the significant regulations to OIRA for review.[75] OIRA has continued to operate under this directive since the Clinton administration, working with agencies to craft the least burdensome regulations, while taking into account the costs that impact all aspects of society.[76]

On January 18, 2011, President Obama announced his intention to renew focus on the job killing impact of onerous, duplicative, and "just plain dumb" regulations that are on the books or in draft form.[77] On January 21, 2011, the President issued Executive Order 13563, which aims to improve the regulatory process and analyze the potential impacts that new regulations would have on job creators.[78]

While the new Executive Order and accompanying memorandum are welcome steps in the right direction, the President's effort does not preclude additional inquiry by the legislative branch. Indeed, the obligation to conduct rigorous oversight into administrative actions that are preventing job creation lies with Congress and is especially necessary because the President's recent statements are not wholly consistent with the actions taken by his Administration. Moreover, while E.O. 13563 appropriately discusses the importance of ensuring that the benefits of a regulation exceed the cost imposed on the private sector, some have raised concerns that the executive order contains a loophole for rules that may not be able to stand on their own. E.O. 13563 states that agencies may:

> consider (and discuss qualitatively) values that are difficult or impossible to quantify, including equity, human dignity, fairness, and distributive impacts.

The terms "human dignity," "equity," and distributive impacts" are undefined. The danger is that this language in the directive could "transform an important tool to check excessive regulation into a way to justify whatever rule" the agency wants.[79]

Over the first two years of the President's term, the federal government issued 132 economically significant regulations (defined as having impacts of $100 million or more per year) – or, on average, 66 major regulations per year. President Obama's upcoming Regulatory Agenda details 183 more regulations than last year at this time.[80] The regulatory road ahead looks even more daunting when one focuses on the largest regulations. The Agenda reveals a 20 percent increase in economically significant regulations, or 40 more regulations with impacts of over $100 million under development now than at this time last year.[81]

Moreover, several respondents to Chairman Issa's inquiry expressed concern that many agencies have found ways to circumvent the regulatory process put in place by statute and preceding Executive Orders. As the National Stone, Sand, and Gravel Association asserts:

> ...agencies' more frequent issuance of 'guidance' that circumvents formal notice and comment rulemakings allows the government to avoid providing needed notice to the regulated and interested publics. This Government failure to provide notice and comment leaves no chance for stakeholders to provide input and/or to assure sufficient time for compliance. 82

Issuing a policy change through a guidance document, as opposed to engaging in the informal rulemaking process, allows an agency to avoid judicial review of agency actions, leaving an aggrieved party without remedy. Other observers have predicted that the Administration will push through via regulation what they were not able to pass through Congress.[83] Accordingly, it is incumbent on Congress to set in motion its own oversight mechanism to assist the President in the identification and improvement of regulations and regulatory processes that impose unnecessary burdens on job creators.

V. Reporting on the Outreach Effort

In furtherance of the committee's obligation to oversee OIRA and agencies, which are responsible for regulations that impose an inordinate burden on job creators, Chairman Issa directed a broad-based outreach effort to collect information and employment data. He requested the information from firms and trade associations of all sizes and in all industry sectors to determine which regulations and administrative processes are negatively impacting private sector job growth. Through this exercise, the preliminary staff report reviews the types of regulations that the private sector identifies as an impediment to recovery. The following sections present the information submitted to the Committee in response to Chairman Issa's request to "examine existing and proposed regulations that negatively impact the economy and jobs." This information will be organized in two ways: section VI will focus on the cumulative impact that regulations have on certain sectors of our economy and section VII will list and explain some of the most frequently cited regulations. The remaining responses, as well as additional Committee analysis, can be found in section A of the appendix.

VI. CUMULATIVE IMPACT OF REGULATIONS

In Executive Order 13563, President Obama pointed out the importance of assessing the cumulative impact of regulations, stating that: "each agency must... tailor its regulations to impose the least burden on society, consistent with obtaining regulatory objectives, taking into account, among other things, and to the extent practicable, the *costs of cumulative regulations*."[84] The cumulative impact of regulations, within an agency and across the government is an important perspective for regulators to incorporate into their burden analysis. After all, job creators do not live in a world where they are only subject to one regulation issued by one agency. Rather, job creators are subject to a myriad of regulations and compliance obligations enforced by the Environmental Protections Agency, the Department of Labor, the Internal Revenue Service, Health and Human Services, and other agencies. Accordingly, in this section, we examine the cumulative impact of certain regulations on four sectors of our economy: utilities, construction, manufacturing, and small business.

A. Utilities

The United States is blessed with some of the lowest industrial electric rates among developed countries.[85] While the recent recession caused energy consumption to decline between 2007 and 2009, dropping 6.84 percent, in order for the economy to rebound, and for the improvement to be sustainable, consumers must have continued access to affordable power.[86] Yet America's utilities are facing considerable hurdles in the form of regulations issued by this Administration. Indeed, the utilities sector offers fertile ground to begin understanding how federal agencies should consider the cumulative impact of regulations, in addition to the cost and benefit of any one particular regulation. Perhaps most significant is the Administration's actions toward coal, which provides 44.5 percent of the electricity generated in America.[87]

The Environmental Protection Agency (EPA) has issued a host of new regulations affecting coal-generated power, directing these plants to purchase costly new equipment for dealing with everything from boilers to plant cooling water intake structures. EPA rules affecting coal include tightened electric generating unit standards, the regulation of greenhouse gases as a pollutant, the reconsideration of Ozone NAAQS, Boiler Heater Maximum Achievable Control Technology (Boiler MACT), as well as increased scrutiny of other emissions[88] . EPA is also proposing a cascade of new standards for already regulated emissions such as nitrogen oxides, sulfur dioxide, and ozone, some of which had their standards updated as recently as 2008.[89] According to a chart provided to the Committee by a utility's industry attorney, from early 2009 to 2017, the industry will have to contend with no less than 35 separate environmental deadlines (see Appendix II). According to the U.S. Chamber of Commerce:

> When several of these massive regulations are piled on top of one another for an industry, the cumulative impact can be overwhelming. The result: industries are effectively regulated out of business. This recently happened for two power plants: Portland Gas & Electric's Boardman coal-fired power plant in Oregon, and Exelon Corporation's Oyster Creek Nuclear Generating Station in New Jersey. In both cases, the utility was forced to choose between installing several hundred million dollars' worth of pollution controls to comply with EPA regulations (regional haze at Boardman, cooling water intake structures at Oyster Creek), or simply shut down early. In both cases, the utility chose to shut down.[90]

Reaffirming this point, in its letter to the Committee, the National Mining Association (NMA) estimates that a suite of regulations for coal-powered electricity generators "could force the retirement of anywhere from 40-100 GW of the existing 310 GW of coal-fueled power plants in a relatively short period of time."[91] Even taking the most conservative figures put forth, this represents a removal of almost 13 percent of the nation's coal-generated electricity from the grid. NMA goes on to estimate that, for those plants not forced to retire, and required to retrofit their facilities, "the capital expenditures have been estimated to exceed $80 billion."[92] A report issued by Credit Suisse found that due to just two EPA rules, the Clean Air Transit Rule and the Maximum Achievable Control Technology (MACT) rule, as much 60 GW of coal power plants will shut down.[93] These rules could have a significant deleterious effect on jobs related to the coal industry, such as electricity generation, rail transport, and mining, to say nothing of the effects on the nation's power supply.

While coal is the epicenter for EPA regulation of the utilities industry, other power sources have not been spared. Nuclear power is also being caught up in this push, notably by potential EPA regulations governing cooling water intake structures at power plants. This potential regulation falls heavily on nuclear power generators, with compliance costs estimated to be between $700 million to $1 billion for nuclear power plants.[94]

Natural gas, which constitutes 23.3 percent of domestic electricity generation,[95] also may be subject to increased regulation. Currently, states are in charge of regulating hydraulic fracturing, in the absence of a Federal regulatory scheme. Yet EPA held hearings in September of 2010 in Binghamton, New York on the subject of the harmful effects of hydraulic fracturing (also known as "fracking"), a process in which liquids are used to release hard to reach gas deposits.[96] This follows a controversial EPA move in which the agency appears to have issued permit-requiring regulations regarding a certain type of hydraulic fracturing without going through the usual regulatory process.[97] Fracking is crucial to accessing enormous deposits of natural gas that cannot be reached with other technology, such as the Marcellus Shale. This source, spanning New York, Pennsylvania, and West Virginia, among other states, is believed to contain 489 trillion cubic feet of gas.[98] EPA's actions thus far could be a precursor to full-blown EPA regulation of this job-creating domestic power resource.

According to a report issued by the North American Electric Reliability Corporation (NERC), a combination of just four specific EPA regulations could have an enormous impact on electricity reliability. The report warned that the United States could lose about 7 percent of its electric capacity if EPA implements regulations on cooling water intake, coal ash disposal, clean air transport, and utilization of maximum achievable control technology (MACT) for air pollutants.[99] In the same report, NERC goes on to recommend that the "pace and aggressiveness of these environmental regulations should be adjusted to reflect and consider the overall risk to the bulk power system."[100]

The utilities industry does not feel pressured by EPA alone. According to the Edison Electric Institute (EEI), utilities are also concerned about the uncertainty regarding new regulatory obligations issued by the Commodity Futures Trading Commission for OTC derivative end-users. EEI represents U.S. shareholder-owned electric companies, and its members serve 95 percent of ultimate electricity customers in the shareholder-owned segment of the industry and represent approximately 70 percent of the U.S. electric power industry.[101] In the case of utilities, the average cash flow impact per company of being miscast as a swap dealer, for instance, "could amount to between $250 million and $400 million per year," which would seriously harm the much-needed capital reserves of utilities.[102]

The cumulative impact of regulations issued by this Administration could restrict currently available sources of base load energy, causing electricity prices to rise. Yet in order for the economy to get back on its feet, reliable and affordable energy is an essential ingredient. This is especially the case for the manufacturing sector, a part of the American economy that is highly reliant on an affordable and predictable power supply.

B. Manufacturing

Recently, President Obama has spoken about the economy and manufacturing. At a stop at a General Electric plant in Schenectady, New York, he remarked: "We want an economy that's fueled by what we invent and what we build. We're going back to Thomas Edison's principles. We're going to build stuff and invent stuff."[103] During his State of the Union speech, he said "We have to make America the best place on Earth to do business."[104] Despite the President's words of support for American manufacturers, his Administration is responsible for implementing policies that have imposed significant new burdens on this struggling sector of the economy. According to research commissioned by the National Association of Manufacturers, "structural costs imposed on U.S. manufacturers including regulation create a 17.6 percent cost disadvantage when compared with nine major industrialized countries."[105] Until recently, the Obama Administration had not shown signs of awareness about the real world impact that onerous regulations had on American manufacturers and the Americans who work for them.

In the last decade, the American manufacturing industry has faced increased barriers to expansion and job creation. Meanwhile, the industry has continued to expand and hire in places like China, India, and Brazil."[106] Today, China is the world's largest provider.[107] Manufacturing is still crucial to the U.S. economy, and the government should seek to foster an economic climate that enables our manufacturers to compete on the world stage.

Chairman Issa has received a wide variety of feedback from members and representatives of the U.S. manufacturing community, ranging from furniture manufacturers to plumbing suppliers to mattress makers. In some cases, the same regulation shows up repeatedly across a range of industries. These more pervasive regulations, such as EPA's boiler emission regulation (Boiler MACT), will be described in-depth in Section VII (C)(1) of the report. However, some regulations are only mentioned by a few specific trade organizations. For these sectors, a specific regulation can mean the difference between hiring more workers and laying people off. This section will review correspondence received by the Committee from various segments of American manufacturing and explain the regulatory burdens that are putting good U.S. jobs in jeopardy.

According to the Brick Industry Association, businesses in their trade create approximately 200,000 jobs in America.[108] However, since the construction downturn began in 2006, approximately 9,000 direct manufacturing jobs, and approximately 86,000 indirect brick jobs in distribution, design, installation and related fields, have been lost.[109] In addition to this hardship, brick makers are facing onerous industry-specific regulations. The first is a re-issuing of a Maximum Achievable Control Technology rule for clay brick and tile (Brick MACT). EPA finalized the original Brick MACT in 2003 to regulate emissions that might be produced when the raw brick materials are fired in kilns to make bricks. The industry spent over $100 million to install and operate required control devices to meet the 2006 compliance date.[110] In 2007, more than a year after enforcement of Brick MACT began; a federal court vacated the rule and the standards in their entirety and sent them back to EPA to be rewritten. EPA is now developing a new Brick MACT but is using the achievements of brick manufacturers under the remanded rule against them as a basis for even more stringent standards. Last year, EPA estimated the revised Brick MACT would cost the industry $188 million per year.[111] Based on figures cited by the Brick Industry Association, brick manufacturers' total revenue in 2009 was approximately $940 million.[112] According to EPA's own estimates, Brick MACT will impose a compliance cost of approximately 20 percent of the industry's revenue, endangering the viability of brick making, and its corresponding jobs, across the United States.

Simultaneously, the Occupational Safety and Health Administration (OSHA) is expected to propose a rule this year, across all industries, to substantially reduce the allowed exposure to crystalline silica in the workplace. However, extensive scientific evidence appears to demonstrate that the risks from exposure to silica from quartz in brick materials are not the same as risks from quartz used in other industrial settings.[113] Decades of studies indicate that illness caused by exposure to crystalline silica is essentially non-existent in brick industry workers.[114] The brick industry is concerned that OSHA is undertaking this regulation without providing an opportunity for input from brick makers, whose industry may not require the new standard since the current standard is already adequately protective of their workers. The increased cost burden of these new requirements, which may not provide any demonstrated health benefit for brick workers, will jeopardize jobs. OSHA has the statutory power to keep the current standard for brick manufacturing, even if they make a new standard for industry in general.[115]

In separate correspondence, the Committee also heard from the NanoBusiness Alliance and the Silver Nanotechnology Working Group. Nanotechnology, as defined by the National Science Foundation, "refers to the ability to manipulate individual atoms and molecules, making it possible to build machines on the scale of human cells or create materials and structures from the bottom up with novel properties. Nanotechnology could change the way almost everything is designed and made, from automobile tires to vaccines to objects not yet imagined."[116] Representatives of nanotechnology manufacturers express frustration regarding EPA's consideration of a requirement that the manufacturers report any adverse effects of any nanomaterial-containing pesticide product—regardless of whether the problems were caused by nanomaterial or not. Because there would be no proof offered or even study of risk associated with nanomaterial, this could create a significant chilling effect on the use of this technology.[117] In fact, some nanotechnology manufacturers have already begun laying off workers and others fear they will soon go out of business because of these regulations.[118] This is an example of how even seemingly minor actions taken by the federal government can have devastating effects on a manufacturing industry.

In some cases, regulations can produce perverse anti-environmental effects, as well as roadblocks for job creation. A prime example of an unintended consequence is regulation facing the scrap recycling industry. The Institute of Scrap Recycling Industries notes that in 2009 the scrap recycling industry recycled 579,568 tons of plastic bottles for export alone.[119] This statistic shows not only the role the industry plays in recycling common waste that would otherwise be destined for landfills, but it also highlights the crucial role recyclers are playing as exporters. In performing these functions, the industry provides an estimated 100,000 jobs.[120] However, a cloud of regulatory uncertainty hangs over this industry. The EPA sets standards for what can be recycled safely and what cannot (and thus will become waste). However, EPA has refused to definitively state whether it would allow recycling of plastic from automobiles or appliances. The industry notes these beneficial economic effects of allowing recycling of these plastics:

- $946.7 million of new spending on equipment;
- $247.9 million of new spending on construction industry services;
- 23,746 new jobs; and
- $1.1 billion of additional gross earnings of employees[121]

The lack of clarity from the federal government causes paralysis in the industry. Without certainty, industrial recyclers say they will not proceed with investment in new facilities, and thus will not create the high-paying jobs that accompany this investment. Moreover, the additional environmental benefits associated with recycling will be foregone.

In some cases, the Administration has proposed a regulatory burden that appears on its face impossible to meet. This example, provided by APA – The Engineered Wood Association, is illustrative;

> In June of 2010, EPA concluded that formaldehyde (FA) causes nasopharynx cancer, all leukemias, myeloid leukemia and lymphohematopoietic cancers as a group... EPA also proposed a maximum FA exposure level of 0.007 ppb, far below naturally occurring levels including exhaled human breath at 2.0 ppb.[122]

Setting a formaldehyde standard below what is found naturally in human breath would seem to be an impossible standard set by the government.

EPA and OSHA are not the only agencies responsible for burdensome regulation. The Plumbing Manufacturers International, which represents companies that make 95 percent of the plumbing products sold in the United States, wrote to the Committee about Department of Energy (DOE) regulations it is facing.[123] Last year DOE rapidly issued a new definition of a showerhead that would unilaterally ban several types of devices. Changing this definition, which had stood for decades, and banning devices is a significant act of regulation. However, DOE only allowed a short 30-day period for the interested parties to offer comments or express concerns with this change.[124]

When industry is weighed down by regulatory compliance burdens, it is hard pressed to create the jobs that the nation needs to get back on its feet. This passage from a letter received by the Committee from the Forging Industry Association sums up the regulatory burdens facing the American manufacturing sector:

> From the U.S. Environmental Protection Agency (EPA) to the Department of Energy (DOE), the Department of Interior (DOI) and the Occupational Safety and Health Administration (OSHA), there appears to be little to no understanding of the manufacturing process and the unintended consequences of certain actions throughout the supply chain. For example, forged parts are critical components of alternative energy sources such as wind turbines and nuclear power plants. However, natural gas and induction furnaces are required to make forged parts. As EPA regulates greenhouse gas (GHG) emissions and potentially requires small and medium sources to comply with GHG emission limits, forging operations may have to comply with these limits solely because they use natural gas in the making of forged parts. So while on one hand the Administration and others trumpet the need for increased use of alternative energy sources, agency proposals are poised to make the very U.S. manufacturers necessary to build those alternative sources less competitive. Similarly, regulations aimed at the oil and gas industry or the automotive or aerospace industries are often proposed without regard to the potentially devastating downstream effects on their suppliers.[125]

Accounts like this increase concern that the Obama Administration has not been looking at the cumulative impact that its numerous silos of regulation have on manufacturers. If the U.S. is going to maintain manufacturing leadership in the world, then there must be hospitable conditions for its revival and growth. The current regulatory climate is hurting this effort.

C. Construction

The construction industry, subject to a number of regulations across several government agencies, has an unemployment rate above 18 percent (double the economy-wide rate). Representatives of the construction industry are concerned about several EPA regulatory proposals, including regulation of GHG's, regulation of Coal Ash, Ozone NAAQS, as well as OSHA regulations, such as the I2P2 program, and IRS's new 1099 reporting requirements.

The construction industry was one of the hardest hit industries following the bursting of the housing bubble and the accompanying recession. In 2009 and 2010, housing starts – the number of new homes on which construction begins within a certain period – were at their lowest levels since 1978, falling almost 1.3 million units within a span of three years.[126] Economists and investors use housing starts as a leading indicator to determine the trend of the overall economy and the construction industry. Thus, a downward trend in housing starts shows both a lag in the economy and the construction industry.

Trade groups representing the construction industry have identified numerous current and proposed regulations that harm economic growth or cause uncertainty for future investment in their industry. The Associated General Contractors of America (Contractors), which surveyed its members and internal experts, is very concerned with EPA's regulation of greenhouse gasses (GHGs). Pursuant to the Clean Air Act, EPA is imposing a permitting scheme on GHG emissions from stationary sources, which many fear could delay the construction of a significant number of projects. The uncertainty created by EPA's permitting scheme for GHGs causes customers of constructions interests to delay or defer the starting date for construction projects.[127]

Similarly, EPA's revision of the National Ambient Air Quality Standards (NAAQS) for Ozone could also have deleterious effects on both ongoing and future construction projects. If finalized, the strict ozone limits EPA is currently considering could dramatically increase the number of regions in non-attainment.[128] This designation will effectively put large swaths of the country off limits to many types of construction because of the equipment required for many projects.[129] Industry groups forecast that this "closing-off effect" on construction projects will seriously deter job creation, not only in the industry itself but also in the manufacturing industry responsible for component parts, the shipping industry, and the other related industries that are closely tied to construction.[130] Furthermore, so long as the region is in non-attainment, it is possible that the emission of ozone by other sources can hinder construction projects even if the construction project is not a major source of ozone.[131]

The companies that supply construction projects also commented on the burden of environmental regulations to their respective industries. The American Architectural Manufacturers Association, representing window, door, and skylight manufacturers, raised concerns about the EPA Lead Renovation, Repair, and Painting Program (LRRP).[132] The LRRP removed "opt-out" provisions for those renovating homes built prior to 1978, thus subjecting such construction projects, and the inputs required to complete those jobs, to regulation under the rule.[133] The changes to this rule increase the costs of projects carried out on pre-1978 structures, discouraging the purchase of new inputs, such as windows or doors, as well as the undertaking of the entire construction project.[134] The lumber industry, whose members supply products to the construction industry, also expressed concerns over the LRRP for many of the same reasons. In addition, they felt EPA constructed an inappropriate implementation scheme and provided an inadequate lead testing system.[135]

Contractors and homebuilders are worried about the LRRP as well. Remodelers predict lost business and even unintended negative health effects because the rule does not apply to homeowners. Because of increased costs, these homeowners may elect to forgo professional services and do remodeling themselves, thus increasing the risk to the population who own older homes.[136] Contractors also have concerns about the rule's application to commercial buildings, when the law was originally intended for residential buildings.[137] The industry feels that this rule would create a perpetual state of testing, training, and certification due to the necessity for "continuous maintenance" at commercial sites – leading to unnecessary costs and project delays.[138]

Finally, EPA's consideration of a rule that would treat coal combustion residuals (CCR), also known as coal ash and fly ash, under the Resources Conservation and Recovery Act (RCRA) as a hazardous waste is cause for great alarm. Fly Ash is an important ingredient of cement. If EPA decrees that the key ingredient is a hazardous waste, there will be severe economic implications for the cement industry, as well as the constructing industry, which requires the widespread use of cement.[139]

In addition to the impact of environmental regulations on job creation within the construction industry, the regulatory burden associated with labor and workplace standards may hinder job creation. The Department of Labor (DOL), through the Occupational Health and Safety Administration (OSHA), has enacted and proposed a number of workplace standards that construction companies, and especially those that are small businesses, find difficult to implement. The industry frequently cites the added costs associated with OSHA compliance mandates and the diversion of capital from production staff to compliance staff needed to satisfy the recordkeeping requirements as barriers to meaningful job creation.

Of particular concern is the Injury and Illness Prevention Program (I2P2), a proposed rule that requires employers to implement specific standards for all safety and health hazards that exist within the construction industry.[140] Both representatives of the construction industry, and those that supply its means of production, worry that this program gives OSHA the ability to issue violations for work conditions that are not currently subject to any specific OSHA standard or rule – leaving the employer in a state of compliance limbo.[141] Since OSHA would be seeking to issue fines for violations currently unregulated by the agency, and not currently existing on the books, this rule exposes construction firms to unknowable levels of legal exposure.[142]

The representatives of the construction industry also cited that the new Form 1099 Requirements, mandated by the Patient Protection and Affordable Care Act, as particularly burdensome to its smallest businesses. The 1099 requirements to be implemented in 2012, requires businesses to file a Form 1099 for all vendors to which they pay more than $600 annually for both goods and services. Some businesses fear such a dramatic increase in paperwork burden from Form 1099 that they foresee the hiring of an additional staffer simply to comply with the rule.[143] The construction industry necessarily works with a large amount of vendors but is not currently required to file a 1099 for all these interactions. Accordingly, compliance with this rule will move resources away from productive labor towards compliance roles.[144]

D. The Regulatory Impact on Small Businesses

Small businesses not only provide the majority of new employment opportunities for Americans but also contribute to the economy as vehicles for innovation. Moreover, small businesses exist in every industry sector and throughout the country. Small business men and women truly represent the foundation of the U.S. economy. When regulations harm small business, they are exceptionally harmful to job growth. Regulatory uncertainty can be potentially lethal to small business as they do not have the economies of scale enjoyed by their larger counterparts to spread the risk and wait out certain administrative decisions. While politicians universally recognize that small businesses are the lifeblood of the American economy, there is some disagreement as to how they should be treated by the federal bureaucracy.

As a general matter, letters received from representatives of small businesses expressed a concern for the rising cost of energy and the expected impact of several EPA regulations. Small businesses cite EPA regulation of GHGs under the Clean Air Act, Ozone NAAQS, and the Boiler Heater Maximum Achievable Control Technology (Boiler MACT) as having the potential to be the most damaging to their ability to create more jobs.[145] Moreover, small businesses that support more than seven million jobs in the oil and natural gas industry,[146] claim the uncertainty created by the Department of Interior's failure to issue a reasonable number of shallow water permits in the Gulf of Mexico is putting these jobs at risk.[147]

According to the National Federation of Independent Businesses (NFIB), their members believe that certification and testing for EPA's LLRP rule will disproportionately affect their operations due to their smaller overheads and staff. [148] Interestingly, EPA recognized that their rule would have significant adverse economic impacts on a substantial number of small businesses in conducting its analysis during the rulemaking process but went forward regardless.[149]

Of particular concern to many small businesses is the "Right to Know" proposed rules of the Fair Labor Standards Act. These provisions require all employers to disclose to all workers whether they are legally considered to be an employee or an independent contractor and to provide the underlying analysis of the method used to compute their salaries. [150] The responsibility of conducting this analysis typically lies with the employer. These employers are concerned that the proposed rule exposes them to possible monetary penalties if they make an error in this calculation and also diverts the owner away from the management and production aspects of the business.[151]

NFIB also expressed concern for what they perceived was a shift at OSHA away from compliance assistance towards investigations and enforcement, as evidenced by OSHA's expanded force of enforcement officers. [152] Many small businesses fear this ramp up in enforcement officers as a sign of things to come, and they fear incurring penalties as they struggle to comply with the various regulations.[153] Similar to the situation with the "Right to Know" requirements, it is the entrepreneur that also serves as the regulatory enforcer – a role that is difficult to perform when so many other tasks need to be fulfilled.[154] Yet, the small business person is very sensitive to enforcement actions because of the limited funds available for both capital investment and legal risk. As the chance of enforcement actions increase, the small business owner may be compelled to invest less and keep on hand additional capital to cover the risk of additional legal exposure.

Finally, representatives for small business reported that both the Musculoskeletal Disorders Recordkeeping Proposed Rule as well as the Noise Control Interpretation Proposal would hinder the ability for small business to grow because of high compliance costs.[155] As previously noted, these rules have been temporarily withdrawn by OSHA for reconsideration.

The Consumer Product Safety Improvement Act received a significant amount of attention from groups that represent important trades. For example, the National Council of Textile Organizations and the International Sleep Products Association both commented that the original intent of this regulation, to combat lead in Chinese toys, would be misapplied to their products, children's clothing and mattresses, and add tremendous costs to businesses.[156] 97 percent of the mattress industry is composed of small businesses, and these businesses would have to bear the burden of expensive retesting of mattresses that the manufacturers have already completed.[157]According to a letter sent by the National Council of Textile Organizations:

> Given the strict manner in which the CPSC has applied its new CPSIA authority, a number of mattress manufacturers have had to retest prototypes they use to make adult-size mattresses that are intended primarily for use by consumers 12 and under. The costs of these flammability tests can range from to $1150 to $2650 per mattress prototype. Depending on the size and product range of a given producer, a typical mattress manufacturer will need to retest between 12 and 42 prototypes to meet this new arbitrary CPSIA rule.[158]

The Computing Technology Industry Association (CompTIA) expressed concern for the impact that Section 511 of the Tax Increase Prevention and Reconciliation Act of 2005 (TIPRA) has on small business.[159] This provision is scheduled to go into effect in January 2012, and requires the government to withhold 3 percent of all payments for goods and services from government contractors. CompTIA notes that this withholding requirement "departs from the traditional scheme of federal tax payments, because the static 3 percent withholding rate bears no relation to anticipated taxable income."[160] The Small Business & Entrepreneurship (SBE) Council agrees that section 511 will raise costs to taxpayers, restrict cash flow for small firms, and drive small businesses away from the government procurement marketplace.[161] Associated Builders and Contractors (ABC) also adds that this withholding rule is "especially onerous for the construction industry" because it will essentially deplete a contractor's profit (construction contractors typically average a profit margin of 2.2 percent).[162]

VII. Agency Analysis

Finally, this preliminary report will focus in on specific regulations that govern labor policy, the agencies that regulate the financial services industry, and the Environmental Protection Agency (EPA). In addition to this analysis, appendences I and II contain additional analysis of regulatory concerns, broken out by industry and by agency. The agencies and regulations that have been selected for more in-depth analysis in the report were chosen based on the volume of responses expressing concern for the economic impact of the regulations or because significant concerns were raised over the agency processes that lead to the regulation. It is beyond the scope of the report to make recommendations for immediate action on these regulations. Rather, this analysis merely reflects the concerns as stated by respondents.

A. Labor Policy

Business organizations have identified multiple proposed regulations and policies issued by the Obama Administration and the Department of Labor that they view as costly, and burdensome inhibitors of job growth. This section will discuss the government actions that regulate labor policy that numerous respondents to Chairman Issa have identified as being onerous and impairing their job creation efforts.

1. OSHA Noise Standards

Last fall, the Occupational Safety and Health Administration (OSHA) issued a proposal to alter workplace noise standards by changing OSHA's interpretation of "feasible administrative or engineering controls." [163] Specifically, OSHA proposed to clarify the meaning of "feasible" to have its ordinary meaning of capable of being done, unless the costs of the controls would be so high as to threaten the livelihood of the business.

Of the numerous labor-specific proposals brought to the Committee's attention, this proposal, by far, generated the most concern from the business community— nearly 30 groups raised it. They assert that OSHA's proposal would reverse decades of agency precedent that currently allows employers to provide their employees with "personal protective equipment," such as ear plugs or ear muffs, instead of more costly administrative or engineering controls, to protect employees from harsh noise.[164] As proposed, employers would not be able to use personal protective equipment unless the company is able to demonstrate that implementing an alternative administrative or engineering control would put the company out of business or threaten its viability.

The American Coke and Coal Chemicals Institute calls the proposal an "unreasonable shift in emphasis" and "stands to add substantial costs...and threatens the global competitiveness of our industry and the industries we supply."[165] Indeed, preliminary estimates from the National Association of

Manufacturers indicate "total compliance costs for fully implementing this proposal may reach billions of dollars."[166] The National Council of Textile Organizations asserts the proposal would be "economically devastating for those smaller-sized manufacturers that make up the bulk of the U.S. textile industry."[167] Finally, the National Tooling and Machining Association, the Precision Machined Products Association, and the Precision Metalforming Association, estimate that these engineering controls "are expected to cost over $10,000 per machine" and the administrative controls "would require shutting down or idling of up to half or more of operating equipment lowering return on investment and decreasing employment."[168]

In addition, numerous groups including the Associated Builders and Contractors, the International Bottled Water Association, the National Concrete Masonry Association, the National Oilseed Processors Association, the Small Business & Entrepreneurship Council, and the Window & Door Manufacturers Association highlight that OSHA is attempting to avoid requirements under the Administrative Procedure Act and other regulatory statutes by characterizing the proposal as a non-regulatory interpretation.[169]

In late January 2011, OSHA recognized many of these concerns and withdrew its proposal to study alternative approaches to limit workplace noise hazards.[170]

2. OSHA Injury Illness and Prevention Program ("I2P2")

OSHA is currently considering issuing a proposed rule to require companies to develop an Injury and Illness Prevention Program ("I2P2").[171] The rule is likely to mandate how companies, both large and small, plan, implement, evaluate, and improve processes and activities that protect employee safety and health. Business groups did not take issue with OSHA's emphasis on workplace safety; instead, they view OSHA's formal program as a mandate that will undermine their current safety programs and lead to inconsistent and unpredictable safety violations by OSHA inspectors.

For example, the National Association of Manufacturers (NAM) fears that the new I2P2 program may not account for effective safety and health programs already in place by many employers and that it would disrupt current safety programs "that have measurable successes."[172] According to NAM, early indications from OSHA signal that the program "may allow OSHA investigators to substitute their judgment of the employer's plan on how to achieve compliance and whether some "injury" in the workplace should have been addressed in some way even if it was not regulated under a specific standard."[173] The National Lumber & Building Material Dealers Association, the National Oilseed Processors Association, the Textile Rental Association, and the American Coatings Association share NAM's concern and believe "efforts made by employers operating effective safety and health programs should not be disrupted by this new mandate."[174] The American Iron and Steel Institute worries that OSHA will use the rule to "double dip" when assessing citations and fines for violations "both covered and not covered by a specific OSHA standard."[175] Indeed, the Associated Builders and Contractors see this as another effort to increase federal control over the private workplace and believes "all employers could find themselves in a never-ending compliance loop as a result of OSHA's rule."[176]

Driving many of these concerns is cost to employers. For instance, the Motor and Equipment Manufacturers Association believes the I2P2 program is "financially unsustainable for businesses of any size to comply."[177] Similarly, the National Federation of Independent Business is worried that "developing a formal program could be a costly exercise for small businesses and become a paperwork nightmare."[178]

3. OSHA Form 300 Musculoskeletal Disorders (MSDs) Column

Early in 2010, OSHA issued a proposed rule to require adding a column to the OSHA Form 300 to record work-related musculoskeletal disorders (MSDs).[179] To some, this may seem like a minor reporting requirement, but many segments of the business community voiced strong reservations about the proposed rule. Associated Builders and Contractors (ABC) argues that changing the form "wrongly groups together a variety of disorders and symptoms that are not necessarily related (noting even the scientific community has been unable to settle on a reliable definition or cause of most MSDs)."[180] They believe adding a hard-to-define, catch-all category could lead to inclusion of erroneous data on the form which may not even be the result of workplace injury.[181] Other business groups fear the new reporting requirement will allow OSHA to use their general duty clause to issue violations in lieu of a national ergonomics standard, which was overturned by Congress using the disapproval resolution in the Congressional Review Act of 2001.[182]

Further, the National Federation of Independent Business (NFIB) claims that OSHA attempted to avoid compliance with the Small Business Regulatory Enforcement and Fairness Act (SBREFA) by severely underestimating the cost of the proposed rule. SBREFA requires OSHA to submit proposals to Small Business Advocacy Review Panels if they will have a significant economic impact on a substantial number of small entities. OSHA estimated that management could read and interpret the new rule within five minutes and correctly identify and record each MSD in one additional minute for each injury. NFIB disputes this. They argue that this estimate "demonstrates OSHA's fundamental misunderstanding of how small businesses operate."[183] In the majority of their membership, the onus is on the small business owner, not a compliance expert, to understand and comply with the new rule. NFIB notes that for a small business owner, "good faith efforts to comply with vague, overly technical, and hard-to-find regulations can require significant time away from the business—time that could be better spent growing the enterprise and employing more people."[184] The Automotive Aftermarket Industry Association and the Society of Chemical Manufacturers and Affiliates expressed similar concerns.[185]

The Administration appears to have temporarily heeded these legitimate concerns. In late January 2011, OSHA announced that it is withdrawing the proposed rule to seek further input from small business.[186]

4. OSHA Consultation Agreements

OSHA issued a proposed rule to revise its regulations under the On-site Consultation Program (OCP).[187] The OCP, administered by OSHA, exists to help small and medium-sized businesses identify workplace hazards, receive advice on compliance with OSHA standards, and assist in establishing safety and health management systems.[188] It is a voluntary program, separate from enforcement, and participating does not result in penalties or citations. The proposed rule would allow compliance officers to proceed with an enforcement visit as a result of a voluntary on-site consultation, as well as conduct an enforcement visit regardless of a company's Safety and Health Achievement and Recognition Programs (SHARP) status. SHARP status recognizes small businesses that operate a superior safety and health management program and exempts their worksite from OSHA programmed inspections as long as they maintain their SHARP status.[189]

The small and medium-sized business community believes the proposed rule is an unnecessary, adversarial action. Until now, they have been accustomed to working in tandem with OSHA on compliance issues. For instance, the International Bottled Water Association (IBWA) deems that the success of the OCP is at least partly "based on the understanding that an employer does not have to worry about being reported to OSHA's enforcement program – information is kept confidential as long as workers are not in imminent danger and the employer agrees to follow the advice."[190] IBWA is concerned that changes to the program may discourage companies from participating in the program at any level for "fear of being subject to additional and unnecessary OSHA enforcement inspections."[191] The American Coatings Association, the American Iron and Steel Institute, the Associated General Contractors, the Motor and Equipment Manufacturers Association, and the Textile Rental Association also believe the rule, if implemented, will create a disincentive for businesses to reach out to OSHA for fear they will be subject to inspection and fines.[192]

Small businesses, like NFIB's members, rely on compliance assistance "because they lack the resources to employ specialized staff devoted to regulatory compliance."[193] NFIB argues "reduction of these key incentives, while at the same time beefing up enforcement, shows that agencies want to levy fines and penalties instead of helping small businesses comply."[194] This businesses fear could ultimately lead to more dangerous workplaces, not safer ones.

5. OSHA Combustible Dust

OSHA is currently considering a proposed rule to devise a combustible dust standard for all industries.[195] OSHA defined combustible dust as "all combustible particulate solids of any size, shape, or chemical composition that could present a fire or deflagration hazard when suspended in air or other oxidizing medium."[196] Business groups are concerned that the proposed standard does not differentiate among industries. For instance, the American Wire Producers Association disagrees with "OSHA's goal to create a "one size fits all" standard with respect to dust generated by very diverse types of manufacturing facilities."[197] They claim that steel dust is neither combustible nor explosive, yet it would still be covered by the rule. The American Iron and Steel Institute and the Non-Ferrous Founders' Society echoed these concerns.[198]

Similarly, the National Lumber and Building Material Dealers Association suggests that such an "ambitious effort may be better served by a more narrowly targeted, perhaps industry-specific focus, identifying high risk settings and determining how best to address the hazards therein."[199] The APA - The Engineered Wood Association and the Kitchen Cabinet Manufacturers Association agree. The American Forest & Paper Association believes the rule "could potentially cost the forest products industry and numerous other industries many millions of dollars in capital expenditures and higher operating costs without materially improving worker safety."[200]

6. Project Labor Agreements

In February 2009, President Obama signed E.O. 13502 to strongly encourage the use of project labor agreements (PLAs) in construction projects in which the total cost to the federal government is $25 million or more.[201] In April 2010, the Department of Defense, General Services Administration, and National Aeronautics and Space Administration issued a final rule implementing the Executive Order.[202] A PLA is a contract awarded only to contractors and subcontractors that agree to recognize unions as the representatives of their employees on that job; use the union hiring hall to obtain workers; obtain apprentices exclusively through union apprenticeship programs; pay fringe benefits into union-managed benefit and pension programs; and obey unions' work rules, job classifications and arbitration procedures. This is significant for the construction industry as 85 percent of the construction workforce has decided not to join a labor union. [203] Accordingly, this policy effectively excludes 85 percent of the industry's workforce from benefiting from government contracts.

The PLAs, and subsequent final rule, are met with skepticism from the private sector. Associated Builders and Contractors (ABC) points out that studies have found that PLA's "increase the cost of construction by as much as 18 percent."[204] These higher costs determine whether a construction company can make additional hires or must make unwanted layoffs. The Associated General Contractors (AGC), who notes that the unemployment rate in construction remains above 18 percent, believes the E.O. has already caused "great upheaval in the federal market, created an environment that is encouraging bid protests, strained relationships between Federal owners and the contracting community, and placed Federal agency career procurement personnel under an inordinate amount of political pressure to meet the Administration's expectation to award more PLAs."[205] In addition, AGC, as well as the Construction Industry Round Table, believe the E.O. is inconsistent with the Competition in Contracting Act, which directs federal agencies to strive to "obtain full and open competition."[206]

B. Regulations Affecting the Financial Services Sector

In reaction to the credit crisis and home mortgage meltdown that led to recession, agencies with responsibility for the financial services sector have dramatically ramped up their rulemaking activities. Much of the current regulatory activity is directly attributable to the implementation of the Dodd-

Frank Wall Street Reform and Consumer Protection Act, the "Dodd-Frank Act." [207] Of the nearly 500 rulemakings stemming from the Dodd-Frank Act that are scattered throughout a number of federal agencies, there is some evidence that regulations affecting the financial services industry may limit the job creation and growth capabilities of U.S. businesses. [208]

The American Financial Services Association (AFSA) brought to Chairman Issa's attention a 2010 study by academics at the George Mason University Law School stating that regulations implemented under the Dodd-Frank Act could reduce economic growth by as much as 4 percent.[209] Similarly, the Commodity Markets Council (CMC) points out that the financial services industry is simply overwhelmed because the July 2011 implementation date set by the Dodd-Frank Act "is so tight, the quantity of rules so large, and the subject matter so complex...". The activities of CMC members "represent the complete spectrum of commercial users of all futures markets, including agriculture." [210]

While it is beyond the scope of the report to discuss all regulations identified by respondents, or required under the Dodd-Frank Act, the report will discuss several of the regulations that were of concern to multiple organizations. Appendix I provides a chart categorizing all the responses received and noting which organization identified the problematic regulation.

1. Dodd-Frank Federal Reserve Board Debit Card Interchange Fees and Routing

The Dodd-Frank Act directs the Federal Reserve to issue rules to set debit interchange fees.[211] The Federal Reserve recently outlined a proposal that would cap debit interchange fees at 12 cents per transaction, which is about half the current market rate.[212] Interchange fees are a per transaction charge paid by merchants to card issuers and are generally viewed as lucrative fees because they are charged by banks to merchants every time a customer swipes a debit card. The fee is typically calculated as a percentage of the purchase being made and essentially represents the amount of each transaction that a debit card's issuer retains.

The Financial Services Roundtable (The Roundtable), the SBE Council, and Credit Union National Association (CUNA) all identified the Federal Reserve's regulation of interchange fees as problematic. According to the Roundtable, a trade association representing 100 of the largest financial services companies, the Federal Reserve Board's proposed regulation of interchange fees through price controls is of paramount concern. The Roundtable estimates that the Board's proposal would "remove an estimated

$15 billion from the financial services marketplace"[213] and hurt small businesses and consumers in the long run.

The SBE Council, with nearly 100,000 members and 250,000 small business activists nationwide, is also concerned that "[p]roposed Federal Reserve rules regarding interchange fees and forthcoming Consumer Financial Protection Bureau (CFPB) regulations... could make a currently challenging problem much worse for small business owners" [214] by further restricting access to, and increasing the cost of, capital and credit for our nation's entrepreneurs. CUNA noted that since 70 percent of credit unions offer debit cards to their members, implementing interchange fee regulations is seen as "the most chilling effect" on the industry.[215] Credit union executives reported that they may be forced to impose monthly checking account fees in the neighborhood of $15-$20.[216]

2. The Consumer Financial Protection Bureau (CFPB)

The Dodd-Frank Act created the Consumer Financial Protection Agency (CFPB) as an independent bureau at the Federal Reserve, with a broad mandate to prohibit unfair, deceptive, or abusive practices with respect to consumer financial products and services. This Bureau was created in response to concerns that the recent economic crisis was caused largely by financial institutions that were not regulated strictly enough.

However, it appears that the language creating this entity was unnecessarily broad and did not adequately define the appropriate scope and role of the Bureau. Respondents who commented on the CFPB are concerned that when the Bureau comes into existence in July 2011 it will have an unprecedented amount of authority to regulate the market for consumer financial products in the years to come. Specifically, the Roundtable cites a 2010 study, which found that future regulatory actions taken by the Bureau, including implementation of most federal financial consumer protection laws, removal of "unfair, deceptive and abusive"[217] consumer lending products, and extensive loan program disclosures on existing products like payday loans, could reduce net job creation by 4.3 percent.[218] The American Financial Services Association (AFSA) is concerned about the autonomous CFPB's "extraordinary authority over all facets of consumer credit" and its shocking lack of congressional oversight.[219] AFSA notes that the Dodd-Frank Act "fails to give any statutory direction to the new CFPB to determine the adequacy of existing state laws and regulations under which these companies operate before imposing new federal burdens."[220] Likewise, DBA International, the "voice for the debt buying industry," [221] is very concerned about the CFPB's new, far-reaching rulemaking authority. They suggest Congress make comprehensive amendments to the existing Fair Debt Collection Practices Act[222](FDCPA) which is the primary statutory authority regulating the debt industry, before the CFPB starts issuing new FDCPA regulations.

3. Dodd-Frank SEC Facilitating Shareholder Director Nominations ("Proxy Access")

The Dodd-Frank Act also extended the rulemaking authority of the U.S. Securities and Exchange Commission. The Business Roundtable (BRT), an association of CEOs from leading U.S. companies, believes that a number of these regulations will be "burdensome and costly" and have a "negative consequence to the economy and jobs."[223]

BRT and its members are particularly concerned about what they see as a new federal right to proxy access created by the SEC. The SEC rule, issued in August, requires companies to include board of director nominees by certain shareholders in their proxy materials.[224] Under the rules, shareholders will be eligible to have their nominees included in the proxy materials if they own at least three percent of the company's shares continuously for at least the prior three years. According to the BRT, the SEC's rule "undermines decades of state law, precedent and organic evolution of corporate law" and could have serious consequences for economic growth and job creation.[225] Accordingly, the BRT and the U.S. Chamber of Commerce sued the SEC in September to vacate the rule.[226] Shortly thereafter, the SEC announced it would delay implementation of the rule pending the outcome of the court challenge.[227]

4. Dodd-Frank SEC Conflict Minerals

On December 15, 2010, the SEC issued a rule that would apply to public companies that use conflict minerals, such as gold, tantalum, tin, or tungsten, for products they manufacture.[228] Under the rule, a company must disclose to the SEC whether its conflict minerals originated in the Democratic Republic of the Congo or an adjoining country.[229] If so, the company is required to furnish a separate report to the SEC as an exhibit that includes a description of the measures taken by the company to exercise due diligence on the source and chain of custody of its conflict minerals.[230] If a company fails to adequately disclose its due diligence efforts to the SEC, it could be liable for violations of Exchange Act Sections 13(a) or 15(d), as applicable (15 U.S.C. 78m(a) and 15 U.S.C. 78o(d))."[231] This rule applies to retailers carrying store-brand products that contain these minerals, as well as to manufacturers and mining interests, regardless of whether the company has any influence over the manufacturing specifications of the product.[232]

The National Electrical Manufacturers Association (NEMA), the Association of Electrical and Medical Imaging Equipment Manufacturers, and the Association of Connecting Electronics Industries (ACEI) all expressed concern regarding the potentially significant impact of the "conflict minerals" regulations on U.S. manufacturers. Although the intent of the regulation is to prevent the atrocities that are occurring in DR Congo, these trade associations are concerned that it will also "cost each U.S. issuing company significant financial and time resources." [233]

Moreover, respondents pointed out that the SEC might not be in the best position to regulate the minerals trade. According to BRT, Section 1504, which requires resource extraction issuers to report payments to foreign governments, and Section 1503 of the Dodd-Frank Act, which relates to disclosure of mine safety violations to the SEC, are "costly requirements" about "unrelated concerns" and "[t]he SEC has no expertise to regulate in this area."[234] IPC notes that the proposed regulations "may cause unnecessary disruptions of the minerals trade."[235] ConocoPhillips, Inc., is likewise concerned about the "[d]isclosure of payments by resource extraction issuers" to the SEC.[236]

5. CFTC Regulations

The Dodd-Frank Act gave the U.S. Commodities Future Trading Commission (CFTC) significant rulemaking authority, which has caused a significant amount of alarm within the private sector. The CFTC set up 30 teams to draft more than 40 rules required under the Dodd-Frank Act. Some observers have expressed concern that there is no team responsible for "facilitating the sharing of salient information between teams," which "ignores the inherent relations that should exist between the rules."[237] The Commodities Market Council (CMC) has expressed concern that the CFTC is using the Dodd-Frank legislation "as an opportunity to propose unnecessary and extremely prescriptive regulations on already regulated derivative markets."[238] CMC is fearful that this abrupt shift from "principles-based to prescriptive regulation" will not serve the industry in competing globally for market share and could impact jobs and growth going forward.

One notable aspect of the Dodd-Frank Act that falls under the purview of the CFTC and has caused a high level of concern in the private sector is the "end-user exception" from the mandatory clearing of swaps.[239] Although the Dodd-Frank Act forces most over-the-counter (OTC) derivatives onto exchanges and through clearinghouses, lawmakers carved out a broad exemption for so-called "end users"- nonfinancial companies in industries like automotives and gas that use derivatives to hedge or mitigate their exposure to commercial risk, which often comes in the form of fluctuations in currencies, interest rates, and the like. [240] However, an ambiguity in the Dodd-Frank Act actually "threatens to undermine the 'end user exemption.'"[241] At issue is whether the CFTC can impose margin requirements on end-users. In other words, the CFTC may be able to force these end-users to put aside a certain percentage of their capital "to provide a cushion for the clearinghouse in the case they fail."[242]

Since an explicitly written exemption stating that end-users are excused from posting margin to trade through clearinghouses did not make it into the final text of the Dodd-Frank Act, some anticipate that the CFTC will interpret its authority to impose costly margin requirements on end-user transactions.[243] This raises the possibility that many in the private sector may have to set aside capital that they would have used for business investment or creating jobs.[244] In February 2010, the Coalition for Derivatives End-Users, which represents about 180 companies and groups including Ford Motor Co., Boeing Co., Procter & Gamble Co. and Walt Disney Co., sent a letter to all U.S. senators stating that "[t]he loss of these important risk-management tools would be detrimental to businesses, the economy and job creation."[245]

The BRT also believes it is critical that end users of OTC derivatives, which account for approximately 10 percent of derivatives use and largely "employ derivatives to manage risk, not create it through speculative trading," should have a clear exemption from margin, capital, and clearing requirements imposed by the Dodd-Frank Act.[246] They point to a 2010 study[247], which finds that a 3 percent margin requirement could result in the loss of 100,000 jobs and tie up an average of $269 million per year per company.

The National Association of Manufacturers (NAM) the largest manufacturing association in the U.S., likewise has a strong interest in the implementation of new rules on OTC derivatives since manufactures in the U.S. are end-users of OTC derivatives that use them to manage risk.[248] In particular, imposing margin requirements on manufacturers would divert companies' financial resources "from much-needed business investment and job retention and creation."[249] NAM therefore believes it is crucial that new regulations on derivatives "include a strong and workable exemption for end-users, like manufacturers, that use derivatives to hedge commercial risk." 250

Finally, ConocoPhillips, the third-largest integrated energy company in the U.S., is concerned about new CFTC "definitions of specific financial transactions" and the CFTC "registration and regulation of 'Swap Dealers' and 'Major Swap Participants'" more generally.[251] Since the CFTC will be developing regulations on commodity markets, the Independent Petroleum Association of America (IPAA), which represents thousands of small-business oil and natural gas producers, is also concerned that they will "impact the availability and cost of hedging."[252] Simply stated, IPPA believes that "any increases in regulatory costs that take capital away from investing in exploration and production will negatively impact job growth in the oil and natural gas industry."[253]

C. The Environmental Protection Agency

Respondents have identified over 60 regulatory actions taken by the Environmental Protection Agency that may have a negative impact on job creation. All of these regulations are listed in appendix A along with the groups that identified the regulations as potential job killers.

The report will provide additional analysis on the regulations that raised concern for multiple organizations. Almost half the respondents who identified EPA regulations, pointed towards the following three rules as job killing regulations: Boiler MACT, GHG regulations, and NAAQS for Ozone. In addition, at least eight groups identified EPA action on Chesapeake Bay Total Maximum Daily Load (TMDL), Cooling Water Intake Structures, Disposal of Coal Combustion Residuals (CCRs), E15 Ethanol Rule, Lead Renovation, Repair, and Painting Program, and NAAQS for Particulate Matter. In addition, due to questions raised over procedural irregularities, this report will provide additional analysis on EPA's Revocation of Appalachian Surface Coal Mining Activities under Clean Water Act Sec. 404.

1. Boiler MACT

More than 20 respondents identified Boiler MACT as a regulation that could pose a significant threat to both job creation and existing jobs. EPA proposed the new Maximum Achievable Control Technology standards for industrial boilers and process heaters (Boiler MACT) in June 2010. EPA estimated the rule would impose capital costs of $9.5 billion and an additional $2.9 billion in annualized costs.[254] The rule as proposed will affect 13,555 boilers and process heaters.[255] The proposal would set stringent emission limits and monitoring requirements for 11 subcategories of boilers, based on fuel type and unit design. These standards, which are intended to address hazardous air pollutant (HAP) emissions, would impose tight limits on five HAP/"surrogate" pollutants: Mercury (Hg), Hydrogen Chloride (HCl), Particulate Matter (PM), Carbon monoxide (CO), and Dioxins/Furans (D/F). In order to comply, operators of coal-fired and biomass-fired units might need to install fabric filters to achieve control of mercury and particulate matter; wet scrubbers to meet limits on hydrogen chloride and other acid gases; replacement burners, tune-ups, and combustion controls for carbon monoxide and organic HAPs; and carbon injection for mercury, dioxins, and furans.[256]

According to analysis performed by the Council of Industrial Boiler Operators (CIBO), EPA dramatically underestimated the cost of the proposed rule. CIBO's analysis predicts that private industry would have to spend about $20 billion up front to comply with the proposed rule, which puts as many as 337,000 jobs at risk, and the rule could reduce GDP by as much as much as $1.2 trillion.[257] Separately, a study conducted by Fisher International estimates the pulp and paper industry costs will be $2.8 billion annually, $17 billion total, and could cause the closure of up to 30 mills, resulting in the loss of 17,000 jobs.[258] The ripple effect from the rule throughout the pulp and paper supply chain and surrounding community escalates the job losses to over 70,000.[259]If these estimates are correct, EPA's initial analysis of cost of $9.5 billion dramatically underestimated the impact of the rule.

The Boiler MACT rule would have a wide ranging impact across industries – which is reflected in the volume and range of responses received. For example, both the American Chemistry Council and the American Forest and Paper Association cited this rule, as well as groups that represent small businesses, such as NFIB, the American Home Furnishings Alliance (AHFA), and the National Oilseed Processors Association. According to the submission of the U.S. Chamber of Commerce, EPA's draft proposal sets hazardous air pollutant emission limits from industrial boilers and process heaters - used by a wide range of manufacturers - at levels, which are barely detectable and possibly unachievable.[260] More specifically, the American Home Furnishings Alliance argued that EPA got the definition of "biomass" wrong. Under the proposal, EPA treats dry wood biomass the same as wet biomass used by other types of boilers. According to AHFA, dry wood biomass burns cleanly, has a neutral CO2 emissions scoring, and has a high heat value. By establishing a single large group of boilers that use both dry wood fuel and wet wood fuel, EPA ignored the benefits and unique characteristics of dry wood boilers.[261] Among other concerns, NFIB pointed out that the continuous testing and monitoring requirements create considerable new paperwork and recordkeeping burdens.[262]

Apparently, since promulgating the draft rule, EPA itself has recognized that its initial approach imposed an unreasonable burden on the economy. According to Gina McCarthy, the Assistant Administrator for Air and Radiation, "When EPA issued the proposal in April, the agency was scrambling to meet a court deadline... and the agency had very little information on some [of the boilers]."[263] "Now that we have the information at hand, it changes the calculation entirely."[264] Based on the new information the agency received in public comments, EPA petitioned the District Court for the District of Columbia for up to 15 months of additional time to complete the rulemaking. Unfortunately, this request was denied. Due to the court's decision, and EPA's aggressive initial proposal, the agency must issue a final Boiler MACT rule by February 20, 2011, and faces the untenable position of finalizing a rule that the agency has admitted to be fatally flawed.

2. Greenhouse Gas Regulations

In a landmark decision, *Massachusetts v. EPA* (2007), the Supreme Court held that greenhouse gasses (GHGs) qualify as air pollutants covered by the Clean Air Act (CAA). The Court further found that the EPA Administrator must determine whether emissions of greenhouse gases from new motor vehicles "cause or contribute to air pollution which may reasonably be anticipated to endanger public health or welfare."[265] In response, EPA issued two final findings regarding the applicability of the CAA to GHGs in December 2009. The first finding was that current and projected concentrations of six key GHGs (carbon dioxide, methane, nitrous oxide, hydrofluorocarbons, perfluorocarbons, and sulfur hexafluoride) in the atmosphere threaten the public health and welfare of current and future generations. This is referred to as the "endangerment" finding. The second finding was that the combined emissions of GHGs from new motor vehicles and motor vehicle engines contribute to the atmospheric concentrations of key greenhouse gases and hence to the threat of climate change. This is referred to as the "cause or contribute" finding.

In 2008, EPA issued an interpretative memo (known as the "Johnson Memo") finding that a pollutant is "subject to regulation" under the federal Prevention of Significant Deterioration (PSD) permit program when it is subject to either a provision in the CAA or becomes subject to a regulation adopted by EPA that requires actual control of emissions of that pollutant.[266] In March, 2010, EPA reaffirmed the Johnson PSD Interpretative Memo and established January 2, 2011, (the effective date of the light-duty vehicle standards) as the date that GHG requirements of the vehicle rule would trigger

CAA permitting requirements for stationary sources.[267] PSD regulations require the installation of the best available control technology (BACT) for new sources and for major modifications of existing sources. Under the CAA, emissions thresholds for criteria pollutants are 100 and 250 tons per year (TPY).[268] In April, 2010, EPA finalized the light-duty vehicle rule controlling GHG emissions and confirmed January 2, 2011, as the earliest date that a 2012 model year vehicle subject to the standards could be sold in the United States.[269]

To be clear, the reaffirmation of the Johnson memorandum and the finalization of the Light-Duty Vehicle Rule worked in tandem to activate the Prevention of Significant Deterioration (PSD) and Title V permitting obligations on stationary sources. Despite strong admonitions by the Office of Advocacy within the Small Business Administration, at no point in the regulatory process has EPA conducted an economic assessment of the impact that the combination of EPA actions have had on the stationary sources that now have to obtain new permits in order to operate.[270]

a. The Tailoring Rule

Under the plain language of the statute, emissions thresholds for criteria pollutants are 100 and 250 tons per year (TPY). At these levels, EPA estimates that 82,000 PSD permits would be required each year and six million facilities would need Title V operating permits.[271] Many commercial establishments, apartment buildings, hospitals and schools could find themselves subject to EPA regulation. In an effort to avoid this immediate result, EPA issued a final rule on May 13, 2010, establishing regulatory thresholds for GHG regulation for stationary sources.

Under the "tailoring" rule, sources already subject to PSD requirements would be required to implement GHG BACT requirements if a modification results in an emissions increase of 75,000 TPY or more of GHGs as of January 2, 2011. Beginning July 1, 2011, to June 30, 2013, PSD permitting requirements will cover new construction projects that emit GHG emissions of at least 100,000 tpy even if they do not exceed the permitting thresholds for any other pollutant. Modifications of existing facilities that increase GHG emissions by at least 75,000 tpy will be subject to permitting requirements even if they do not significantly increase emissions of any other pollutant. Operating permits will be required for facilities that emit at least 100,000 tpy of GHGs. EPA may begin to require permits for smaller sources as of April 30, 2016.

Numerous organizations, ranging from American Farm Bureau to the Business Roundtable, to the SBE Council, cited uncertainties surrounding the tailoring rule as a significant source of concern. Accordıng to comments from the Agricultural Retailers Association, it is not clear to them that, "EPA has the authority to tailor through omitting certain emitters from the rule requirements." These retailers fear that "their farmer customers and their businesses will eventually be brought into the rule. The cost of complying with sourcing permits would cause many customers to stop farming and would [be] detrimental to most retail facilities." 272 The Brick Industry Association expressed similar concerns. While their association represents employers of approximately 200,000 Americans, they noted that approximately 9,000 direct manufacturing jobs and approximately 86,000 indirect brick jobs in distribution, design, installation and related fields have been lost since the construction recession began in 2006.[273] According to this group, "the groundwork is set for smaller sources such as brick kilns to be regulated in the next few years. The brick industry could be quickly enveloped, resulting in lengthy permit review processes as states struggle to keep pace with the new permitting requirements. While EPA may ultimately require little or no change to brick operations, particularly because more than 80 percent of brick kilns are fired by natural gas, significant permitting delays will stifle job creation and the industry's recovery."[274]

Finally, the Forging Industry Association, which represents approximately 500 forging operations, mostly small businesses, in 38 states, Canada, and Mexico stated, "While EPA's decision to start with large stationary sources means forgers only currently have to worry about the potential effect of these regulations on its suppliers in the metals industry, we are very concerned about future regulation of smaller sources."[275] Forging is one of the oldest known metalworking processes, where metal is pressed, pounded, or squeezed under great pressure into high-strength parts known as forgings.

b. PSD Permits, BACT Guidance

On November 10, 2010, EPA issued its long awaited Best Available Control Technology (BACT) Guidance (Guidance Document) for state permitting agencies to use as they attempt to move forward with PSD permits, taking into account GHG emissions. The Guidance Document is supposed to inform both industry and the states what GHG control technologies must be deployed before an applicant may receive a PSD permit. If a company is unable to obtain a permit, they will not be able to construct or significantly modify their facilities.

While EPA had originally pledged to release the guidance document last June, the materials were not published until November 10, 2010. In addition to this long delay, EPA provided the public only 14 days to comment on the voluminous material. Several organizations have criticized EPA's failure to provide adequate lead time as adding to the uncertainty that discourages needed capital investment.[276] These concerns are shared by the non-partisan Congressional Research Service, which states that, "With a multi-billion dollar investment in a project designed to operate for decades at stake, the lack of a definitive [control] option arguably adds more uncertainty to future coal-fired power plants."[277]

In addition to uncertainty, organizations such as the American Iron and Steel Institute (AISI), whose member companies account for 80 percent of both U.S. and North American steel capacity, point out that the technical document, published separately for the steel industry, contains a number of misstatements and inaccuracies.[278] According to AISI, EPA documents did not reflect the true status of existing and emerging technologies for the industry and, accordingly, have heightened the industry's concerns with the regulations.[279] For example, EPA asserts in the document that the iron and steel industry can further reduce energy use by 27 percent for integrated mills and 53 percent for electric arc furnaces plants.[280] However, AISI countered "several of the technologies identified in the Technical Document have already been adopted by the industry. For example, many integrated facilities already control coal moisture, utilize pulverized coal injection, and have improved blast furnace control systems. Similarly, many electric arc furnaces commonly employ foamy slag practices, oxy-fuel burners, insulation of furnaces, and walking beam furnaces."[281]

c. Greenhouse Gas and Fuel Efficiency Standards

EPA and the Department of Transportation (DOT) have issued a series of regulations to set Corporate Average Fuel Economy (CAFE) standards for both light duty and heavy-duty vehicles. The first in the series, which set fuel economy/GHG rules for light-duty vehicles between model years 2012-2016, was part of the so-called "historic national agreement" between the State of California, EPA, DOT, and the auto industry. This is also the regulation, which set in motion the requirement that stationary sources obtain PSD permits for GHGs. However, representatives for stationary sources were not present at the negotiating table and EPA has never analyzed the economic impact on the broader economy resulting from their regulatory action. According to NADA, the GHG fuel efficiency standards exceed Congressional mandates and require duplicative agency involvement when one rule (issued by NHTSA) would have provided a superior public policy outcome.[282] According to NADA, this rule will distort the market by forcing manufacturers to build vehicles whether or not there is public demand for them.[283]

With respect to the EPA/DOT joint proposal for GHG and Fuel Efficiency Standards for Heavy Duty Vehicles, the Owner-Operator Independent Drivers Association (OOIDA) has criticized the "command and control" approach taken by the Administration.[284] OOIDA represents the interests of small business trucking professionals and professional truck drivers throughout the United States and Canada and is comprised of nearly 155,000 members nationwide. OOIDA is concerned that the proposal will significantly increase the cost of newer heavy-duty vehicles, perhaps even increasing the purchase price of those vehicles beyond what many small businesses can afford.[285] Moreover, this group believes that much less costly ways to achieve the goals of increased fuel efficiency and GHG reduction have been ignored.[286] The Motor and Equipment Manufacturers (MEMA) expressed concern about the impact and feasibility of future mandates addressing heavy-duty vehicles beyond model year 2019.[287]

While supportive of the initial joint rulemaking for light duty vehicles, the Auto Alliance, including Toyota and Ford Motor Company under separate letter, expressed some concern for the Administration's approach to setting the second round of fuel efficiency standards. According to the Auto Alliance, the key concern is the potential for state regulations that would undermine the ongoing effort to develop a single national program for motor vehicle fuel economy standards in the 2017-2025 model years (MY).[288] Specifically, they were concerned that the California Air Resources Board (CARB), which has received a special waiver from EPA to regulate GHGs from mobile sources, intends to pursue the development of its own separate rules for MY 2017-2025 light-duty vehicles.[289] While it appears CARB has since backed off, it had previously indicated that proposed new state GHG regulations covering model years 2017-2025 would be issued in the spring 2011, well in advance of the process underway at NHTSA and EPA.[290] It is important to note that beyond MY 2016, CARB must receive a waiver from EPA for their GHG laws to be enforceable against auto manufacturers, pursuant to Section 209 of the CAA. The 2009-2016 California GHG rules received such a waiver of preemption from EPA in June 2009.

3. National Ambient Air Quality Standards (NAAQS)

Under the Clean Air Act (CAA), EPA has the authority to set National Ambient Air Quality Standards (NAAQS) for several different substances and correspondingly restrict industrial emission of these substances. EPA is directed under the statute to review each NAAQS level every five years, for six widespread pollutants. EPA is in various stages of reviewing all six standards although there is no corresponding mandate to change the standard after each review. Once a new NAAQS is issued, a lengthy timeline begins for states to bring their affected non-attainment areas into compliance with the new standard. If EPA finds that a state is not complying, it can take over the process from the states and institute a "federal implementation plan" where EPA runs the compliance process. EPA can even go so far as to deny the state benefits such as federal highway funding. EPA is not required to take the economic cost of compliance into consideration when adjusting the NAAQS.[291]

Respondents expressed a widespread concern with EPA's approach to reviewing and revising NAAQS for two substances in particular: ozone and particulate matter (PM).

a. NAAQS for Particulate Matter

The NAAQS for Particulate Matter (PM NAAQS) are actually two separate standards, one for smaller or "fine" particles known as $PM_{2.5}$, and another for larger or "coarse" PMs, known as PM_{10} -- the numbers being based on the size thresholds, in micrograms, of the particles. EPA studies and releases the updated standards for both PM levels concurrently. While some states are still working to achieve the mandated levels of PM that EPA set in 1997, EPA is currently in the process of revising its PM standard and has said it will release its proposal in June 2011.

Several groups expressed concerns over EPA's intention to lower the PM2.5 standard, which would mean more stringent controls for fine particle precursors, *i.e.*, sulfur and nitrogen oxides, as well as carbon monoxide. The 24-hour standard for PM2.5 is set at 35 micrograms and the annual standard is set at 15 micrograms. EPA has yet to articulate its proposal for fine Particulate Matter NAAQS; however, there is reason to believe the agency is considering rules that would lower the 24-hour standard to 30 micrograms and the annual standard to 11 micrograms.[292] More stringent PM standards will increase the number of cities and towns designated as "non-attainment."

The American Forest & Paper Association explains that the current standard is already very strict and that compliance with increased standards could cost their industry $5 billion to comply.[293] It notes lingering concerns about the science used to justify a lower standard.[294] The U.S. Chamber notes that lowering the standard "could put hundreds of counties into non-attainment, jeopardizing economic growth."[295] According to the American Coke and Coal Chemicals Institute (ACCCI), the mere threat of this more stringent regulation has caused one of its member companies to delay a new $700 million coke plant with over 120 new jobs and an annual payroll, including benefits, of $8 million.[296] ACCCI represents 100 percent of the producers of the nation's metallurgical coke and 100 percent of the nation's producers of coal chemicals derived from byproducts of coke-making. Coke is an essential raw material for the production of iron and steel.[297]

The Committee also heard concerns about EPA's plans to increase the stringency of the coarse particulate matter standard (PM_{10}). Through this rule, EPA would attempt to regulate sources of coarse crustal fugitive dust emissions. EPA and its scientific advisory committee are recommending a reduction in the NAAQS for PM_{10} from the present level of 150 to either 65 or 75 micrograms of dust per cubic meter of air.[298]

Various stakeholders have pointed out that these PM_{10} levels can be caused by factors that do not fit into the traditional areas of emission regulation, and accordingly would be very difficult to reduce. The American Farm Bureau points out that "coarse particulate matter is much more prevalent in rural areas due to unpaved roads, working farm fields, and blowing winds."[299] The National Stone, Sand and Gravel Association (NSSGA) makes similar observations about the non-industrial nature of coarse particulates: "Most of the PM_{10} dust is generated from windblown dust from uncontrollable sources such as arid un-vegetated surfaces in rural areas, unpaved roads, and dry land farming and tilling. Industrial sources of PM_{10} are very small compared to these natural, municipal and agricultural sources."[300]

Because of the nature and sources of coarse particulate matter, it is almost impossible for industrial sources of PM_{10} to sufficiently reduce their emission levels without crippling their business. For example, the NSSGA mentions one of their member companies would have to cut production by two-thirds to come into compliance with the considered regulation, which would have a devastating impact on the company's workforce.[301] The association goes on to mention the effect that EPA's proposed action could have on road building: "Taken further, this cut in aggregate production would lead to a shortage of stone, concrete, and asphalt for state and federal road building/repair, commercial and residential construction, which in turn would cause an increase in the price of stone for these projects ranging from 80 percent to 180 percent and further suppress employment in the construction industries."[302] Such a cost increase will cut deeply into the amount of capital that these companies will have available for hiring new workers.

b. NAAQS for Ozone

Chairman Issa received over twenty separate pieces of correspondence identified EPA's consideration of Ozone NAAQS as a prime source of concern. EPA has taken an even more aggressive regulatory stance over the Ozone NAAQS than PM NAAQS.

In 2008, EPA reduced the Ozone NAAQS from 80 parts per billion (ppb) to 75 ppb. As mentioned above, under the Clean Air Act, EPA is expected to review NAAQS levels every five years, and tighten standards if the body of scientific evidence requires a stricter standard to protect public health and the environment.[303] However, in the case of the ozone NAAQS, less than two years after moving from 80 ppb to 75 ppb, EPA proposed to lower the standard further, to levels between 60-70 ppb.[304] At EPA's own admission, there is no new science driving this decision. "In this reconsideration, EPA is not relying on studies about the health and ecological effects of ozone that have been published since the science assessment to support the 2008 review was completed."[305] Accordingly, EPA is considering finalizing this rule three years earlier than appropriate and the decision was not based on the emergence of new science.

The large volume of responses is likely due to studies, which indicate that lowering the standard to 70 ppb would create 515 non-attainment areas in the states and a standard of 65 ppb would apply to 608 regions of non-attainment.[306] This is a massive increase in the geographic areas that would be put on "EPA probation." For ozone nonattainment areas, control measures require reductions in NOx and VOC emissions. Additionally, any new major sources of NOx and VOCs must "offset" their emissions and install technology that achieves the "lowest achievable emissions rate" without consideration of costs.

Compliance costs associated with the proposed lower standard are also overwhelming. The U.S. Chamber of Commerce cites a study indicating that it will cost $1.013 *trillion* annually between 2020 and 2030 and a potential loss of 7.3 *million* jobs by 2020.[307] This is a staggering blow, representing a 5.4 percent net reduction in GDP and 4.3 percent of the projected labor force.[308]

4. Chesapeake Bay Total Maximum Daily Load

The Chesapeake Bay Total Maximum Daily Load (TMDL) is an EPA action pursuant to the Clean Water Act that requires waterways in the Chesapeake Bay watershed to comply with specific water quality standards to abate pollution.[309] EPA may implement a TMDL when it determines a waterway has unacceptable pollution levels.[310] A TMDL requires that the jurisdictional states of the watershed create Water Implementation Plans (WIPs) detailing how each state plans to comply with the pollution standards set by EPA.[311] With regard to the Chesapeake Bay TMDL, the affected states are Delaware, Maryland, New York, Pennsylvania, Virginia, West Virginia, and the District of Columbia. The Chesapeake Bay TMDL sets pollution reduction levels for nitrogen, phosphorus, and sediments in these states, which WIPs regulate for those listed pollutants. The current WIPs include pollution reduction measures such as building wastewater treatment plants, implementing state agricultural regulations, and increasing enforcement for runoff of these pollutants.[312] The Chesapeake Bay TMDL is the result of planning and research over the past ten years, with EPA and the states first beginning the process in 2000.[313] Currently, the states are in the process of establishing the second phase of WIPs pending EPA approval.[314]

Private sector concerns regarding the Chesapeake Bay TMDL hinge on the scope and feasibility of the standards imposed by EPA on the state regulating authorities and the level of transparency provided by EPA in disclosing the science of its underlying study.[315] The American Farm Bureau, a trade association that represents farm and ranch families, worries about an "unprecedented" action that "may well allow EPA to dictate virtually all economic activity including the ability to build roads, homes and grow food" within the Chesapeake region.[316] Groups representing agricultural interests are very concerned about the inability of the industry to comply with such stringent water controls.[317] The Agricultural Retailers Association, a trade group that represents businesses that supply American farmers, sent the following comments: "EPA has adopted thoroughly unachievable goals for water quality in the Bay region, given the population that lives there and the environmental impact of supporting and employing a growing number of residents."[318]

The American Forest and Paper Association (AFPA) is a trade association that represents the wood products, paper and packing, and forestry industries. Their concerns regarding the Chesapeake Bay TMDL deal with forest product facilities and the water discharge levels that they produce.[319] AFPA believes that in order to meet the TMDL pollutant levels, the measures would "go beyond the limits of existing technology and therefore likely [be] unachievable."[320] The National Alliance of Forest Owners, an association that represents private forest owners many of which are in the timber industry, recognizes the potential for added costs because of the TMDL and worries that the federal government will overstep the bounds of the CWA by regulating non-point sources instead of the states.[321]

The Responsible Industry for Sound Environment (RISE), a trade group that represents non-agricultural uses of fertilizers and pesticides, fears that the TMDL could lead to an outright ban on the personal use of such products, harming manufacturers and the small businesses that use and sell fertilizers.[322] Moreover, RISE is concerned that regulations will severely impact the many small businesses involved in the lawn maintenance industry if municipalities, attempting to comply with the stringency of the WIPs, curtail the use of pesticides or fertilizer within the Chesapeake Bay watershed.[323] This industry group is particularly concerned that the burden of TMDL regulations will disproportionately fall on the industries conducting business in the Chesapeake Bay region hindering job growth and economic expansion.[324]

5. Cooling Water Intake Structures

The breadth and scope of EPA's upcoming regulations is not limited to greenhouses gases. Ten organizations—mostly from the energy sector—expressed concern about the proposed EPA regulations governing water intake structures at power plants and some manufacturing facilities. These plants and facilities use cooling water taken from a source such as a lake or a stream to generate electricity and maintain their equipment at safe and efficient temperatures. Under the Clean Water Act, cooling water intake structures must reflect the best technology available (BTA) to minimize adverse environmental impacts.[325] By March 14, 2011, EPA is expected to propose regulations of existing facilities' water intake systems. These regulations "will likely apply to all existing and new nuclear and fossil steam generating units, which contributed over 93 percent of 2008 U.S. generation."[326]

As stated earlier in the utilities section, the nuclear power sector will be heavily impacted by EPA's proposed regulations of cooling water intake structures. But the nuclear sector is not alone. Respondents, such as the American Iron and Steel Institute, the Electric Reliability Coordinating Council, and the Industrial Energy Consumers of America, are worried that the forthcoming rules will impose extremely stringent standards, forcing plants to decide between costly updates or shutting down.

The major concern is whether EPA will require "open-loop" or "once-through" cooling systems to switch to "closed-loop" cooling systems.[327] Although EPA requires newly built cooling water intake structures to use closed-loop systems, approximately 43 percent of U.S. electric power plants use open-loop cooling systems.[328] If EPA requires existing facilities to adopt closed-loop systems, the retrofit costs could dramatically increase compliance costs for the utilities industry. As the American Petroleum Institute stated, "potential retrofit costs could be significant, and could affect energy supply and reliability." The North American Electric Reliability Corporation estimated that the costs of the rules could cause 32,500-36,000 MW of capacity to be vulnerable to retirement.[329]

Respondents hope that EPA will consider the severe economic impact of forcing existing plants and facilities to change to closed-loop cooling water systems. EPA Administrator Lisa Jackson has acknowledged that a closed-loop cooling technology "may not be available at every plant."[330] She further stated that she does "not favor a one-size-fits-all federal mandate." Hoping EPA will keep this pledge, Edison Electric Institute has urged EPA "to keep the rule reasonable and flexible, recognizing constraints on existing facilities."[331]

6. Coal Combustion Residuals

Coal combustion residuals (CCRs), often referred to as "coal ash," are different solid and liquid by-products created during the burning of coal. The by-products have commercial value and are used to make cement, concrete, wallboard, and road building materials. In fact, 43 percent of CCRs are reused for such purposes.[332]

CCRs are currently regulated by the states with essentially no federal involvement. However, on June 21, 2010, EPA announced that it will begin reconsideration of how to treat CCRs under the Resource Conservation and Recovery Act (RCRA) when they are disposed in landfills or surface impoundments. The agency is considering two options: classification of CCRs as hazardous under subtitle C of RCRA or as a solid waste under RCRA subtitle D.[333]

Managing CCRs as hazardous waste would dramatically affect coal-fired power generation. In a letter to Chairman Issa, the U.S. Chamber of Commerce pointed to a study that predicts the early retirement of 388 to 2,000 megawatts of coal-generated electricity, equaling 12 to 53 coal plants, if coal ash is regulated as a hazardous pollutant.[334] The substantial costs of handling coal ash as hazardous waste would be insurmountable for many power plants.

Furthermore, if these plants are no longer able to sell these materials to industries that beneficially use coal ash, then an important revenue stream for these power generators will be lost. Forcing this much power generation offline would also significantly impact energy costs and hurt the economy.

In addition to the affect on utilities, the classification of CCRs as hazardous waste could also harm the industries that use coal ash to make their products. Fly Ash is an important ingredient in cement, and the cement industry currently obtains coal ash from the utilities that burn the coal in the first place. According to research commissioned by the Portland Cement Association, U.S. cement consumption is expected to at least double from 70 million metric tons in 2010 to 147 million in 2025.[335] Additionally, fly ash is predicted to become a larger per-unit part of cement - growing from10.5 percent of cement mix to 14 percent-15 percent by 2030.[336] However, with the implementation of EPA's hazardous waste rule alone, the Association estimates that construction costs could increase by 4 percent-11 percent, due to the increased cost of cement.[337]

Respondents are concerned about a damaging consumer backlash against purchasing products made with hazardous waste, even if EPA does not consider that end product to be hazardous. Their argument is that no one will want to live in a house made of materials derived from hazardous waste, even if EPA says that it is okay to use that waste for building materials. The hazardous classification will have a strong chilling effect on the market for safe products containing coal ash.

Not only will this rule negatively affect the already beleaguered coal industry and its workers (please refer to Section VI(A)on utilities), but it will translate into higher costs for electricity consumers and the jobs that require access to dependable and reasonably-priced power. For example, respondents, such as the American Forest and Paper Association, are worried that they will pay increased electricity costs if EPA classifies CCRs as hazardous waste.[338] Furthermore, the potential harmful effects of increased CCR regulation on cement making and construction are significant. EPA has considered this matter before. In 2000, the agency decided against regulating the substances as "hazardous waste" under subtitle C of RCRA.[339] It is clear that respondents affected by this regulation hope the Obama Administration will keep these factors in mind as EPA considers, again, whether to classify CCRs under subtitle C.

7. E15 Ethanol Rule

In March 2009, EPA acquiesced to a petition filed by Growth Energy and 54 ethanol manufacturers to allow the introduction of 15 percent ethanol by volume in gasoline (E15).[340] The petition called for EPA to act under section 211(f) of the Clean Air Act, waiving the prohibition on ethanol above 10 percent by volume in gasoline.[341] EPA granted a waiver on the prohibition of ethanol for use in model year (MY) 2001 and newer light-duty motor vehicles under specific conditions regarding the sale and use of E15 to prevent consumer misfueling.[342] The studies conducted by EPA found that use of E15 fuel in MY2001 and newer vehicles will not cause these vehicles to exceed exhaust emissions standards, providing grounds for EPA to grant the waiver.[343] The conditions placed on the sale of E15 gasoline are as follows: all parties involved in the manufacture and sale of E15 are to submit a plan addressing the conditions of the waiver for EPA approval, retail dispensers must provide labels on gasoline indicating use only for MY2001 and newer motor vehicles, product transfer documents must accompany all transfers of fuels for E15 use, and parties must participate in compliance surveys regarding the labeling requirements for E15 fuels.[344] It remains unclear as to the exact method by which E15 will be sold to consumers (through separate pumps similar to diesel gasoline is the assumption); yet, industry groups still worry about its implementation. This action is currently in litigation in federal court.

EPA waiver raises concern among industry groups and companies for various reasons. The major issue regarding the waiver is the method used by the agency in carrying out the safety tests for E15 with regard to older vehicles.[345] Whereas the federal government requires the manufacturing industry to submit all of its vehicles to the government for testing, EPA's testing of E15 only looked at the impact on a small sample of potentially affected vehicles rather than all makes and models.[346] The auto industry does not support this one-size-fits-all approach to such a sweeping agency action.[347]

Another concern is the safety of E15 for use in older engines, despite EPA's research with regard to the increase in ethanol.[348] The National Automobile Dealers Association (NADA) feels that the E15 "content level is in excess of manufacturer design specifications [and] could dramatically impair vehicle and emissions performance and even damage the vehicle itself."[349] Furthermore, NADA raises concerns that auto retailers will bear the burden of dealing with motorist dissatisfaction should the E15 damage automobiles, thus leading to potential harm in sales.[350] Toyota commented on the concern of the level of alcohol this rule would allow in gasoline.[351] Toyota supports the addition of ethanol into gasoline, however, suggests that EPA rule lacks the "proper lead time provided to automobile manufacturers."[352] Toyota further comments that this rule "expos[es] millions of owners of existing vehicles to potential problems with their vehicles due to use of a fuel that their vehicles were not designed to use."[353]

Automobile manufacturers worry that consumers may experience major problems with their vehicles leading to potential engine and catalytic converter failures. [354] Due to the uncertainty of the method of sale of E15, industry groups speculate that in the event of misfuelings that damage vehicles, serious tension between consumers and manufacturers will harm the ability of auto manufacturers to market their products.[355] Moreover, the National Petrochemical and Refiners Association (NPRA) raises concerns about the negative effects on non-road engines: "studies show gasoline blends containing more than 10 percent ethanol could lead to engine damage in older vehicles and non-road engines, such as those in chainsaws, lawnmowers, boats, and snowmobiles."[356]

The National Marine Manufacturer's Association (NMMA) claims that E15 could inappropriately attract customers because its potentially lower price point will leave consumers looking for a cheaper option without knowing it could harm their engine.[357] For boat engine owners that use E15 instead of gasoline approved for such engines, NMMA surmises a damaged boat engine would cause a number of consumers to leave the boating market because of steep cost of replacement in a strained economy.[358] NMMA feels that "the loss of a boat engine will likely mean the loss of a lifetime of boating, and thus loss of a lifetime customer, as replacing equipment in difficult economic times will be more unlikely."[359]

8. Lead Rule

In 2008, EPA promulgated the Lead Renovation, Repair and Painting Rule (LRRP) pursuant to section 402(c)(3) of the Toxic Substances Control Act (TSCA) to address lead-based paint hazards in housing and child-occupied facilities built before 1978.[360] The rule requires that any renovation work that disturbs an area more than six square feet in size on the interior of a pre-1978 home to follow certain lead work practices supervised by an EPA-certified renovator and performed by an EPA-certified firm.[361] In May 2010, EPA removed the "opt-out" provision from the LRRP that exempted the renovating firm from certain requirements of the rule where the firm retains certification that no child under the age of six resides in the renovated home.[362]

In the same Federal Register Notice, EPA also required renovation firms to provide copies of compliance documentation along with training and work practice requirements of the LRRP rule to residence owners.[363] Also in May 2010, in settling petitions by environmental and children's groups, EPA issued an advanced notice of proposed rulemaking regarding renovations to public and commercial buildings other than those that were child-occupied under the same guidelines as the residential programs.[364] That month, EPA also proposed a rule under LRRP for the cleanup of projects that generate lead dust, requiring testing on the completion of these renovations.[365]

Despite sharing EPA's objective of protecting children and pregnant women from lead hazards, industry groups recognize that the revocation of the "opt-out" provision in the LRRP rule negatively impacts renovation projects.[366] The American Architectural Manufacturers Association (AAMA), a trade association that represents over 250 window, door, and skylight manufacturers and industry related suppliers, maintains that "[a]s renovators began to inform homeowners of the additional remodeling costs now associated with renovations, window sales in some parts of the country plunged by 20 percent."[367] AAMA, along with other groups, urged EPA to reconsider the changes to the "opt-out" provisions and cited a Small Business Advocacy letter arguing that EPA "...failed to perform needed outreach and failed to examine seriously several regulatory alternatives..."[368] Furthermore, a coalition of construction and renovation related industry groups (coalition) asserts that the increased cost of hiring certified contractors "means that legitimate businesses that are complying with the LRRP Rule cannot compete for much-needed work against non-compliant contractors that...lack the training [sic] to actually perform lead-safe renovations and prevent lead hazard exposures."[369]

The coalition cites a number of costs that befell renovators and their surrounding industries upon implementation of the LRRP. First, the LRRP did not present enough opportunities for renovators to become EPA-certified by the start of implementation.[370] Second, lead test kits produced over 60 percent false positive readings, causing an EPA estimated $200 million in unnecessary compliance costs for firms.[371] Finally, EPA's failure to accurately gauge the cost of this rule on small business detrimentally impacted that business sector.[372]

The Associated General Contractors of America (AGC) is a trade association that represents the construction industry. AGC raises concerns about the LRRP rule relating to the "opt-out" provision. Their issue regards the one-size-fits all approach to the advance notice of proposed rulemaking extending the LRRP rule to commercial and public building renovations.[373] The trade group feels that "simply taking residential rules and applying them to commercial buildings will mean a never-ending cycle of lead paint testing, contractor certification, worker training, and comprehensive management practices – all increasing the cost of construction."[374] The coalition is concerned that the EPA stepped outside of the framework of TSCA by considering a new rule without conducting a separate study of lead paint hazards in public and commercial buildings instead of relying on the residential data.[375]

The proposed rule to add clearance testing to the LRRP for both residential and commercial renovation projects concerns the National Lumber and Building Material Dealers Association (NLBMDA).[376] NLBMDA states, "These regulations immediately threaten the recovery of our residential construction and renovation markets and the many jobs associated with construction and renovation."[377] Furthermore, this association calls for "[a] more narrow and tailored approach..." to this regulating scheme.[378]

9. Clean Water Act (CWA) Permitting

On January 13, 2011, EPA issued a Final Determination on the use of three tributary waters as a disposal site for dredge or fill material in connection with the construction, operation, and reclamation of the Spruce No. 1 Surface Mine in Logan County, WV.[379] This Final Determination withdraws and prohibits for future use a lawfully issued and approved for renewal permit by the U.S. Army Corps of Engineers (Corps), held by Spruce No. 1 Surface Mine for coal mining at the site.[380] EPA undertook its action pursuant to section 404(c) of the Clean Water Act (CWA), the "veto clause," which authorizes the agency to prohibit specification of any defined area as a disposal site.[381] EPA invoked the veto clause based on guidance documents released in 2009 that significantly redefine the criteria for evaluating section 404 discharge permits as well as enhance EPA's role in the process.[382]

Industry notes two major issues of concern with this action. First, the National Mining Association (NMA) argues that the broad changes implemented by EPA for section 404 permitting through guidance documents are legislative rules promulgated in violation of the Administrative Procedure Act (APA) because they represent a substantive change to prior regulations not submitted to the notice and comment process.[383] Industry groups also argue that EPA violated its statutory authority mandated by Congress under the CWA by expanding its role in the 404 permitting process to the detriment of the Army Corps.[384] The U.S. District Court for the District of Columbia, in a matter brought by NMA, ruled that an action challenging EPA on both the

APA and CWA violations would succeed on the merits but denied NMA's claim for preliminary injunction.[385]

NMA cites uncertainty for the future of coal mining as a negative impact of this action: "EPA's Guidance amounts to a de-facto moratorium on the issuance of coal mining permits by rewriting the underlying statutory and regulatory permitting framework."[386] NMA reports that a ban on valley fills, such as the one used at Spruce Mine No. 1, would "result in the loss of thousands of jobs and hundreds of millions of dollars of income in West Virginia alone."[387] Moreover, EPA's actions create a feeling of uncertainty amongst a broad-range of trade groups whose members rely on CWA permits, known as the Water Advocacy Council (WAC), representing many sectors of the American economy.[388] These industries, ranging from manufacturing to realty, expressed concern that EPA's actions are negatively impactful on investment in production and job growth and result in a barrier to recovery from the recession.[389] WAC states that "[t]he implications [of the EPA permitting scheme] could be staggering reaching all areas of the U.S. economy."

VIII. Conclusion

This preliminary staff report, identifying regulations that potentially impose impediments to job creation, represents the beginning of a dialogue between this Committee, the Executive Branch, and the American people about steps we can take to help spur job creation and help put Americans back to work. At minimum, the regulatory actions identified in this report merit additional scrutiny to ensure that the processes used to implement these rules are transparent, that the agencies have provided adequate opportunity for stake holder participation, and that the agencies have taken all reasonable steps to minimize the cost of compliance for America's job creators.

APPENDIX I. REGULATIONS BY AGENCY

ENVIRONMENTAL PROTECTION AGENCY	
REGULATION/STATUTES/POLICIES	ORGANIZATION/BUSINESS
Atrazine (Herbicide) Re-Evaluation (Potential): The EPA began a re-evaluation of Atrazine in 2009 although not due for re-evaluation until 2013. Atrazine is an agricultural herbicide primarily used on corn, sorghum, and	American Farm Bureau Federation
Boiler & Process Heater Maximum Achievable Control Technology (MACT) (Boiler MACT), 75 Fed. Reg. 32682 (proposed April 29, 2010) (to be codified at 40 C.F.R. pts. 60, 63, and 24): This rule addresses emissions from boilers, process heaters, and solid waste incinerators. On December 7, 2010, EPA sought an extension of time from the District Court for the District of Columbia to re- propose and finalize these standards.	Air-Conditioning, Heating and
	The Aluminum Association
	American Chemistry Council
	American Coatings Association
	American Coke and Chemicals Institute
	American Forest and Paper Association
	American Home Furnishings Alliance
	American Iron and Steel Institute
	APA—The Engineered Wood Association
	Business Roundtable
	Chamber of Commerce
	ConocoPhillips, Inc.
	Council of Industrial Boilers
	Industrial Energy Consumers of America
	Kitchen Cabinet Manufacturers
	Metal Treating Institute
	Motor and Equipment Manufacturers
	National Asphalt Pavement Association
	National Association of Manufacturers
	National Black Chamber of Commerce
	National Federation of Independent
	National Mining Association
	National Oilseed Processors Association
	Small Business & Entrepreneurship
	Society of Chemical Manufacturers and
	Textile Rental Services Association
Brick and Ceramic Kilns Maximum Achievable Control Technology (MACT) (Potential)	The Aluminum Association
	Brick Industry Association

ENVIRONMENTAL PROTECTION AGENCY	
REGULATION/STATUTES/POLICIES	ORGANIZATION/BUSINESS
California Clean Air Act Pre-emption Waiver, 76 Fed. Reg. 5368: California agreed not to enforce its motor vehicle Greenhouse Gas (GHG) rule in exchange for EPA granting a waiver and issuing CAA regulations for new motor vehicles.	Chamber of Commerce
	National Automobile Dealers Association
Central Appalachian Coal (CAPP): Review of Appalachian Surface Coal Mining Activities under Clean Water Act Section 404, National Environmental Policy Act (NEPA), and the Environmental Justice Executive Order (E.O. 12898): On April 1, 2010, the EPA issued three documents that seek to impose specific conductivity limits on discharges from valley fills that would ensure in-stream conductivity levels do not exceed 300-500 uS/cm.	American Coke and Chemicals Institute
	Industrial Energy Consumers of America
	National Mining Association
	National Sand, Stone, and Gravel Association
Chesapeake Bay Total Maximum Daily Load (TMDL): On December 29, 2010, EPA established the TMDL, a comprehensive "pollution diet" with rigorous accountability measures to initiate sweeping actions to restore clean water in the Chesapeake Bay and the region's streams, creeks and rivers. The TMDL is the largest ever developed by EPA and encompasses 64,000 square-mile watershed.	Agricultural Retailers Association
	American Farm Bureau Federation
	American Forest and Paper Association
	Associated General Contractors
	The Fertilizer Institute
	Industrial Energy Consumers of America
	National Alliance of Forest Owners
	Responsible Industry for a Sound Environment
Chemical Manufacturing Area Source Standards Final Rule 40 C.F.R. § 63 (2009): Finalized on October 29, 2009, this rule establishes national emission standards for air pollutants from "area" chemical manufacturing sources.	Society of Chemical Manufacturers and Affiliates

Table Continued.

ENVIRONMENTAL PROTECTION AGENCY	
REGULATION/STATUTES/POLICIES	ORGANIZATION/BUSINESS
Clean Water Act Section 404(c) "Veto Authority" 33 U.S.C. 1344(c): authorizes EPA to prohibit, restrict, or deny the discharge of dredged or fill material at defined sites. Opponents of the mining in the area of the Pebble Project have requested the EPA to prohibit under 404(c).	Pebble Project
Cleaning Products Claims Policy under the Federal Insecticide, Fungicide, and Rodenticide (FIRFA) 7 U.S.C. 136 et seq. (1996): Change in EPA guidance regarding cleaning of mold and mildew stains	American Coatings Association
	Biotechnology Industry
Comprehensive Environmental Response, Compensation, and Liability Act (CERCLA) Section 108(b)—Financial Responsibility Requirements, 75 Fed. Reg. 816 (proposed Jan. 6, 2010) (to be codified 40 C.F.R. pt. 320): EPA has discretionary authority to impose financial responsibility requirements on industrial sectors "consistent with the degree of risk associated with the production, transportation, treatment, storage, or disposal of hazardous waste."	Industrial Energy Consumers of America
	National Mining Association
	NTMA Precision
	Precision Machined Products Association
	Precision Metalforming Association
Concentrated Animal Feeding Operations (CAFOs) and NPDES Permits (Potential): EPA working on regulations that are expected to require small- and medium-sized CAFOs to obtain NPEDES permits as well as mandating use of more aggressive	American Farm Bureau Federation

ENVIRONMENTAL PROTECTION AGENCY	
REGULATION/STATUTES/POLICIES	ORGANIZATION/BUSINESS
Cooling Water Intake Structures (Clean Water Act Section 316(b)) (Potential): EPA is developing regulations under the Clean Water Act Section 316(b) that requires the location, design, construction and capacity of cooling water intake structures reflect the best technology available for minimizing adverse environmental impact.	American Iron and Steel Institute
	American Petroleum Institute
	Business Roundtable
	Chamber of Commerce
	ConocoPhillips, Inc.
	Council of Industrial Boiler Owners
	Edison Electric Institute
	Electric Reliability Coordinating Council
	Industrial Energy Consumers of America
	National Mining Association
Draft Guidance for Pesticide Registrants on Pesticide Drift Labeling (Pesticide Spray Drift), 74 Fed. Reg. 57166 (proposed on Nov. 4, 2009): EPA proposed guidance for new pesticide labeling to reduce off-target spray and dust drift.	Agricultural Retailers Association
	National Alliance of Forest Owners
Dioxin in Soil Recommended Interim Preliminary Remediation Goals: the EPA developed draft interim preliminary remediation goals to assess the human health risks from exposures to dioxin in soil.	American Chemistry Council
Disposal of Coal Combustion Residuals (CCRs) Proposed Rule, 75 Fed. Reg. 35127 (proposed June 21, 2010) (to be codified at 40 C.F.R. pt. 257, 261, 264 et al.): EPA proposed on June 21, 2010 to regulate for the first time coal ash (coal combustion residuals) to address the risks from the disposal of wastes generated by electric utilities and independent power producers.	American Forest and Paper Association
	Associated General Contractors
	Chamber of Commerce
	Council of Industrial Boiler Owners
	Edison Electric Institute
	Electric Reliability Coordinating Council
	Industrial Energy Consumers of America
	Murray Energy Corporation
	National Association of Home Builders
	National Concrete Masonry Association
	National Mining Association
	National Sand, Stone, and Gravel
	Portland Cement Association

Table Continued.

ENVIRONMENTAL PROTECTION AGENCY	
REGULATION/STATUTES/POLICIES	ORGANIZATION/BUSINESS
E15 Ethanol Fuel Rule (EPA420-F-11-003): On October 13, 2010, the EPA granted a waiver for E15 fuel (blend of 15% ethanol and 85% gasoline) to be used cars and light trucks manufactured between 2001 and 2006.	American Land Title Association
	American Petroleum Institute
	Association of International Automobile
	ConocoPhillips, Inc.
	Grocery Manufacturers Association
	Mazda
	National Automobile Dealers Association
	National Marine Manufacturers
	National Petrochemical and Refiners
	Small Business & Entrepreneurship
	Toyota Motor North America
Effluent Limit Guideline Rule for Construction Site Runoff, 40 C.F.R. § 450 (2009): EPA issued a final rule on December 1, 2009 regulating stormwater discharges from construction and development industry.	Associated Builders & Contractors
	Associated General Contractors
	Council of Industrial Boiler Owners
	Independent Petroleum Association of
	National Association of Home Builders
	National Sand, Stone, and Gravel
Effluent Limitation Guidelines and New Source Performance Standards for the New Airport Deicing Category, 74 Fed. Reg. 44676 (proposed Aug. 28, 2009) (to be codified at 40 C.F.R. pt. 449): EPA is establishing new technology-based guidelines and standards for the discharges from airport deicing efforts.	Air Transport Association
Emergency Planning and Community Right-to-Know Act (Region 4 interpretation of the Fertilizer Retailer Exemption)	Agricultural Retailers Association

ENVIRONMENTAL PROTECTION AGENCY	
REGULATION/STATUTES/POLICIES	ORGANIZATION/BUSINESS
Endocrine Disruptor Screening Program for Chemicals (EDSP): EPA announced the initial list of chemicals to be screened for their potential effects on the endocrine system on April 15, 2009 and the first test orders were issued on October 29, 2009. EPA then developed a second list of chemicals for screening and published three related Federal Register Notices on November 17, 2010.	Consumer Specialty Products Association
	The Methanol Institute
Formaldehyde Emission from Pressed Wood Products, 73 Fed. Reg. 73620 (advanced notice of proposed rulemaking, Dec. 3, 2008) (to be codified to 40 C.F.R. Chapter I): pursuant to the Formaldehyde Standards for Composite Wood Products Act, EPA must promulgate regulations to implement this law by January 1, 2013.	Composite Panel Association
	Kitchen Cabinet Manufacturers Association
Greenhouse Gas (GHG) Emission Tailoring Rule, 40 CFR § 52, 70 (2009): this final rule includes a step-by- step implementation strategy issuing federally-enforceable permits to the largest, most environmentally significant sources beginning January 2, 2011.	Agricultural Retailers Association
	American Coke and Chemicals Institute
	American Farm Bureau Federation
	American Forest and Paper Association
	American Iron and Steel Institute
	American Petroleum Institute
	APA—The Engineered Wood Association
	Chamber of Commerce
	ConocoPhillips, Inc.
	The Fertilizer Institute
	Industrial Energy Consumers of America
	Metal Treating Institute
	Murray Energy Corporation
	National Alliance of Forest Owners
	National Association of Home Builders
	National Black Chamber of Commerce
	National Electrical Manufacturers
	National Oilseed Processors Association
	National Petrochemical and Refiners
	Portland Cement Association

Table Continued.

ENVIRONMENTAL PROTECTION AGENCY	
REGULATION/STATUTES/POLICIES	ORGANIZATION/BUSINESS
Greenhouse Gas (GHG) Emissions Regulations under the Clean Air Act including: Fuel Economy Greenhouse Gas Rules for MY 2012- 2016: on April 1, 2010, the EPA and the Department of Transportation's National Highway Traffic Safety Administration (NHTSA) issued a final rule to establish greenhouse gas (GHG) and corporate average fuel economy (CAFE) standards for light-duty vehicles. Fuel Economy Greenhouse Gas Rules (Proposed) for MY 2017-2025: on January 24, 2011, the EPA along with the Department of Transportation and the state of California announced a single timeframe for proposing fuel economy and greenhouse gas standards for MY 2017- 2025 cars and light-trucks. Greenhouse Gas (GHG) and Fuel Efficiency Standards for Heavy-Duty Vehicles: in response to a Presidential Memorandum of May 21, 2010, the EPA with the National Highway Traffic Safety Administration (NHTSA) announced they will initiate a rulemaking to reduce GHG emissions for commercial medium- and heavy-duty trucks.	Alliance of Automobile Manufacturers
	American Bakers Association (General)
	American Iron and Steel Institute (BACT)
	American Petroleum Institute (NSPS)
	Associated Builders & Contractors
	Association of American Railroads
	Brick Industry Association (NSPS)
	Business Roundtable (NSPS, BACT)
	Chamber of Commerce (General)
	Charlotte Pipe and Foundry Company
	Council of Industrial Boiler Owners
	Electric Reliability Coordinating Council
	Ford (MY 2017-2025)
	Forging Industry Association (General)
	Independent Petroleum Association of
	Industrial Energy Consumers of America
	Motor and Equipment Manufacturers
	Murray Energy Corporation (General)
	National Automobile Dealers Association
	National Black Chamber of Commerce
	National Council of Textile Organizations
	National Petrochemical and Refiners
	National Stone, Sand, and Gravel
	Owner Operator Independent Drivers Association (Heavy-Duty Vehicles)
	Small Business & Entrepreneurship
	Toyota Motor North America
Hydrogen Sulfide as a Hazardous Air Pollutant (Potential)	American Coke and Chemicals Institute
	Independent Petroleum Association of
	Industrial Energy Consumers of America

ENVIRONMENTAL PROTECTION AGENCY	
REGULATION/STATUTES/POLICIES	ORGANIZATION/BUSINESS
Integrated Risk Information System (IRIS) Review of Inorganic Arsenic (Draft Review): the EPA published the toxicological review of inorganic arsenic on February 19, 2010, which addresses only cancer human health effects that may result from chronic exposure.	National Mining Association
Integrated Risk Information System (IRIS) Review of Formaldehyde—Inhalation Assessment (Draft Review): On June 2, 2010, EPA released the draft assessment, which addresses both non-cancer and cancer human health effects that may result from chronic inhalation exposure.	APA—The Engineered Wood Association
	Kitchen Cabinet Manufacturers Association
Integrated Risk Information System (IRIS) Review of Methanol (Draft Review): EPA released an external review draft in January 2010 for public review and comment, which addresses both non-cancer and cancer human health effects that may result from chronic exposure.	The Methanol Institute
Interstate Transport Rule, 75 Fed. Reg. 45210 (proposed Aug. 2, 2010) (to be codified at 40 C.F.R. pt. 51, 52, 72, 78, and 97): this rule would require significant reductions in sulfur dioxide and nitrogen dioxide emissions that cross state lines.	Chamber of Commerce
	Council of Industrial Boiler Owners
	Electric Reliability Coordinating Council
	Industrial Energy Consumers of America
	Murray Energy Corporation
	National Mining Association
Lead Clearance and Clearance Testing Requirements for the Renovation, Repair, and Painting Program (Proposed) 75 Fed. Reg. 38959 (proposed July 7, 2010) (to be codified at 40 C.F.R. pt. 745): EPA requires contractors to perform "dust-wipe testing" after most construction activities to show that lead levels comply with EPA standards.	Associated General Contractors

Table Continued.

ENVIRONMENTAL PROTECTION AGENCY	
REGULATION/STATUTES/POLICIES	ORGANIZATION/BUSINESS
Lead: Renovation, Repair, and Painting Program, 40 C.F.R. § 745 (2008): beginning April 22, 2010, contractors performing renovation, repair and painting projects that disturb lead-based paint in homes, child care facilities, and schools built before 1978 must be certified and must follow specific work practices to prevent lead contamination.	Air Conditioning Contractors of America
	American Architectural Manufacturers
	Associated Builders & Contractors
	Associated General Contractors
	Chamber of Commerce
	Electronic Security Association
	Hearth, Patio, & Barbecue Association
	Insulation Contractors Association of
	Manufactured Housing Institute
	National Apartment Association
	National Association of Home Builders
	NAIOP, the Commercial Real Estate
	National Federation of Independent
	National Lumber & Building Materials
	National Multi Housing Council
	National Glass Association
	Plumbing-Heating-Cooling Contractors—
	The Real Estate Roundtable
	Vinyl Siding Institute
	Window & Door Manufacturers
Mandatory Reporting of Greenhouse Gases (GHG) Rule, 40 C.F.R. § 98 (2010): this rule requires reporting of greenhouse gas (GHG) data and other relevant information from large sources and suppliers in the United States.	American Forest and Paper Association
	Association of Equipment Manufacturers
	Conoco-Phillips, Inc.
	Industrial Energy Consumers of America
	Portland Cement Association
Nanopesticide Policy (Proposed): EPA proposed a nanopesticide policy in April 2010, which requires the presence of a nanomaterial in a registered pesticide to be reported under the "unreasonable adverse effect" provision of FIFRA.	Silver Nanotechnology Working Group

ENVIRONMENTAL PROTECTION AGENCY	
REGULATION/STATUTES/POLICIES	ORGANIZATION/BUSINESS
National Ambient Air Quality Standards (NAAQS) for Lead 40 C.F.R. § 58 (2008): in October 2008, EPA substantially reduced the NAAQS for lead. EPA made final revisions to the ambient monitoring requirements for measuring lead in the air on December 14, 2010.	Non-Ferrous Founders' Society
National Ambient Air Quality Standards (NAAQS) for Nitrogen Oxide 40 CFR §§ 50, 58 (2010): On January 22, 2010, the EPA strengthened the NAAQS for nitrogen dioxide.	American Coke and Chemicals Institute
	American Farm Bureau Federation
	American Iron and Steel Institute
	Associated General Contractors
	Council of Industrial Boiler Owners
	Electric Reliability Coordinating Council
	Industrial Energy Consumers of America
	Portland Cement Association
National Ambient Air Quality Standards (NAAQS) for Ozone, 75 Fed. Reg. 2938 (proposed Jan. 19, 2010) (to be codified at 40 C.F.R. pt. 50, 58): EPA is lowering the NAAQS for the ozone to somewhere in the 60-70 parts per billion range. On December 8, 2010, the EPA Administrator requested more input from agency's science advisors. EPA intends to set a final standard by the end of July, 2011.	American Coatings Association
	American Coke and Chemicals Institute
	American Forest and Paper Association
	American Iron and Steel Institute
	American Petroleum Institute
	APA—The Engineered Wood Association
	Associated General Contractors
	Brick Industry Association
	Business Roundtable
	Chamber of Commerce
	Charlotte Pipe and Foundry Company
	Conoco-Phillips, Inc.
	Consumer Specialty Products Association
	Council of Industrial Boiler Owners
	Electric Reliability Coordinating Council

Table Continued.

ENVIRONMENTAL PROTECTION AGENCY	
REGULATION/STATUTES/POLICIES	ORGANIZATION/BUSINESS
	Industrial Energy Consumers of America
	Metal Treating Institute
	Murray Energy Corporation
	National Association of Home Builders
	National Association of Manufacturers
	National Black Chamber of Commerce
	National Federation of Independent
	National Oilseed Processors Association
	National Petrochemical and Refiners
	Portland Cement Association
	Small Business & Entrepreneurship
National Ambient Air Quality Standards (NAAQS) for Particulate Matter (Potential): EPA will propose NAAQS for particulate matter in early 2011, with final regulations due in 2012.	Agricultural Retailers Association
	American Coke and Chemicals Institute
	American Farm Bureau Federation
	American Forest and Paper Association
	American Iron and Steel Institute
	Chamber of Commerce
	Charlotte Pipe and Foundry Company
	Council of Industrial Boiler Owners
	Electric Reliability Coordinating Council
	Industrial Energy Consumers of America
	National Asphalt Pavement Association
	National Sand, Stone, and Gravel
	Portland Cement Association
National Ambient Air Quality Standards (NAAQS) for Sulfur Dioxide 40 C.F.R. §§50, 53, 58 (2010): EPA strengthened the NAAQS for sulfur dioxide on June 2, 2010	The Aluminum Association
	American Coke and Chemicals Institute
	American Iron and Steel Institute
	Council of Industrial Boiler Owners
	Industrial Energy Consumers of America
	Portland Cement Association
National Emission Standards for Hazardous Air Pollutants (NESHAPs) from the Portland Cement Manufacturing Industry 40 CF.R. §§ 60, 63 (2010): regulates emission limits for mercury, THC, and particulate matter from new and existing kilns located at major sources.	Cemex
	Portland Cement Association

ENVIRONMENTAL PROTECTION AGENCY	
REGULATION/STATUTES/POLICIES	ORGANIZATION/BUSINESS
Navigable Waters Guidance: EPA issued a guidance document under review at the Office of Management and Budget (OMB).	American Farm Bureau Federation
	Chamber of Commerce
New Source Performance Standards (NSPS) for Portland Cement Plants 40 C.F.R. §§ 60, 63 (2010): regulates emission limits for particulate matter, nitrogen oxides, and sulfur dioxide for facilities that commence construction, modification, or reconstruction after June 16, 2008.	Cemex
	Portland Cement Association
Non-Hazardous Materials that are Solid Waste (proposed April 29, 2010) (to be codified at 40 C.F.R. pt. 241): this rule seeks to clarify which non-hazardous secondary materials are or are not solid wastes when burned in combustion units.	American Home Furnishings Alliance
	Automotive Aftermarket Industry
	Chamber of Commerce
	Industrial Energy Consumers of America
	IPC, The Association Connecting
	Non-Ferrous Founders' Society
Numeric Nutrient Water Quality Criteria for Florida Waters, 40 C.F.R. §131 (2010): the final rule published on December 6, 2010, issues numeric water quality criteria for nitrogen/phosphorus pollution to protect aquatic life in lakes, flowing waters, and springs within Florida	Agricultural Retailers Association
	American Forest and Paper Association
	CF Industries
	The Fertilizer Institute
	Industrial Energy Consumers of America
Polychlorinated Biphenyl (PCBs) Analytical Method: PEA has proposed an analytical test method that measures in a very low range of parts per quadrillion.	American Forest and Paper Association

Table Continued.

ENVIRONMENTAL PROTECTION AGENCY	
REGULATION/STATUTES/POLICIES	ORGANIZATION/BUSINESS
Pesticide Permits—Proposed Clean Water Act National Pollutant Discharge Elimination System (NPDES) Pesticide General Permit Program, 75 Fed. 13468 (proposed June 4, 2010): Proposed permit system that will be put in place by April 9, 2011.	Agricultural Retailers Association
	American Farm Bureau Federation
	Responsible Industry for a Sound Environment
Prior Converted Croplands: EPA (with Army Corps of Engineers) recapturing prior converted croplands (PCC) (wetlands drained before 1985 that no longer exhibit the characteristics of wetlands) by altering guidance to claim a "change of use" places PCC under the Clean Water Act.	American Farm Bureau Federation
Residual Risk Reviews of the Pulp and Paper Industry: Pursuant to a settlement agreement, EPA must propose its residual risk determination for pulp and paper mills by June 15, 2011.	American Forest and Paper Association
Safe Drinking Water Act: Hydraulic Fracturing Regulation (Potential)	Conoco-Phillips, Inc.
	Independent Petroleum Association of America
Spill Prevention, Control, and Countermeasure (SPCC) Regulation, 40 C.F.R. § 112 (2008): This rule's purpose is to help facilities prevent a discharge of oil into navigable waters or adjoining shorelines.	American Farm Bureau
	Associated General Contractors
Spruce Mine Clean Water Act Permit (Revocation): for the first time, EPA revoked a previously issued permit in January 2011.	Chamber of Commerce
	National Sand, Stone, and Gravel Association

ENVIRONMENTAL PROTECTION AGENCY	
REGULATION/STATUTES/POLICIES	ORGANIZATION/BUSINESS
Texas Air Permits: Approval and Promulgation of Implementation Plans; Texas; Revisions to the New Source Review (NSR) State Implementation Plan (SIP); Flexible Permits, 40 C.F.R. § 52 (2010): EPA is proposing disapproval of submittals from the State of Texas, through the Texas Commission on Environmental Quality (TCEQ) to revise the Texas SIP to include a new type of NSR permitting program, Flexible Permits (the Texas Flexible Permits State Program or the Program).	Chamber of Commerce
	National Petrochemical and Refiners Association
Toxic Release Inventory (TRI) Articles Exemption Clarification Proposed Rule, 74 Fed. Reg. 42625 (proposed Aug. 24, 2009) (to be codified at 40 C.F.R. pt. 372): EPA is proposing to remove a paragraph of guidance dealing with releases due to natural weathering of products, and is proposing an interpretation of how the articles exemption applies to the Wood Treating Industry, specifically to treated wood that has completed the treatment process.	American Wire Producers Association
	Independent Petroleum Association of
	NTMA Precision
	Precision Machined Products Association
	Precision Metalforming Association
Toxic Substances Control Act (TSCA) Chemical Action Plans 15 U.S.C. §2601 et seq. (1976): In September 2009, EPA announced a comprehensive strategy for chemical management including "action plans" for 12 chemical families.	Grocery Manufacturers Association
	Society of Plastics Industry
Toxic Substances Control Act (TSCA) Proposed Rule to amend the Inventory Update Rule (IUR) 75 Fed Reg. 19830 (proposed Aug. 13, 2010) (to be codified at 40 C.F.R. pt. 704, 710, 711): EPA is proposing to amend the reporting requirements.	American Coatings Association
	Industrial Energy Consumers of America
	IPC, The Association Connecting
	Society of Plastics Industry

Table Continued.

ENVIRONMENTAL PROTECTION AGENCY	
REGULATION/STATUTES/POLICIES	ORGANIZATION/BUSINESS
Toxic Substances Control Act (TSCA) Nanoscale Materials/Products Regulation: To ensure that nanoscale materials are manufactured and used in a manner that protects against unreasonable risks to human health and the environment, EPA is pursuing a comprehensive regulatory approach under TSCA.	NanoBusiness Alliance
Toxic Substances Control Act (TSCA) Proposed Test Rule For Coal Tar and Coal Tar-Derived Chemicals	American Coke and Chemicals Institute
	Society of Plastics Industry
Use of Settlement Agreements: EPA has entered into settlement agreements with environmental organizations, impacting industry outsides the Administrative Procedure Act (APA) rulemaking process.	American Farm Bureau
Utility Boilers Maximum Achievable Control Technology (MACT) (MACT for Power Plants) (Potential): Pursuant to a 2009 consent decree, the EPA must issue a proposed rule new National Emission Standard for Hazardous Air Pollutants (NESHAP) regulation HAP emissions from coal- and oil-fired electric generating units by March 16, 2011 and finalize the rule by November 16, 2011.	Business Roundtable
	Electric Reliability Coordinating Council
	Industrial Energy Consumers of America
	National Mining Association

FINANCIAL SERVICES AGENCIES	
REGULATION/STATUTES/POLICIES	ORGANIZATION/BUSINESS
Dodd-Frank CFTC Portfolio Reconciliation, and Portfolio Compression Requirements for Swap Dealers and Major Swap Participants 75 Fed. Reg. 81519 (proposed Dec. 28, 2010) (to be codified at 17 C.F.R. pt. 23): The CTFC issued a proposed rule to prescribe standards for swap dealers and major swap participants related to the timely and accurate confirmation, processing, netting, documentation, and valuation of swaps. The proposed rules would establish requirements for swap confirmation, portfolio reconciliation, and portfolio compression for swap dealers and major swap participants.	Commodity Markets Council
Dodd Frank CFTC Registration of Swap Dealers and Major Swap Participants 75 Fed. Reg. 71397 (proposed Nov. 23, 2010) (to be codified at 17 C.F.R. pts. 3, 23, 170): the CFTC issued a proposed rule to establish the process for registering swap dealers and major swap participants. The proposal would require swaps entities to become members of the National Futures Association and to confirm that persons associated with them are not subject to a statutory disqualification under the Commodity Exchange Act.	ConocoPhillips
Dodd-Frank CFTC Position Limits for Derivatives, 76 Fed. Red. 4752 (proposed Jan. 26, 2011) (to be codified at 17 CFR Parts 1, 150, 151): the CFTC issued a proposed rule to simultaneously establish position limits and limit formulas for certain physical commodity futures and option contracts executed pursuant to the rules of designated contract markets (DCM) and physical commodity swaps that are economically equivalent to such DCM contracts.	Commodity Markets Council
	Independent Petroleum Association of America

Table Continued.

FINANCIAL SERVICES AGENCIES	
REGULATION/STATUTES/POLICIES	ORGANIZATION/BUSINESS
Dodd-Frank SEC Shareholder Approval of Executive Compensation and Golden Parachute Compensation 17 C.F.R. §§ 229, 240, 249 (2011): On January 25, 2011, the SEC issued a final rule relating to shareholder approval of executive compensation and "golden parachute" compensation arrangements required under Dodd-Frank.	American Express
	Business Roundtable
Dodd-Frank CEO Pay Ratio Disclosure: Dodd-Frank will require all U.S. public companies, companies that are not publicly traded but have public debt, and other companies required to file reports with the SEC to disclose the following compensation metrics: the annual total compensation of the chief executive officer; the median annual total compensation for all employees (except the chief executive officer); and a ratio of these two metrics.	American Express
	Business Roundtable
Dodd-Frank & the Fair Debt Collection Practices Act, Pub. L. No. 109-351, §§ 801–802, 120 Stat. 1966 (2006): Dodd-Frank transferred the Federal Trade Commission's rulemaking authority under the Fair Debt Collection Practices Act to the Consumer Financial Protection Bureau.	DBA International
Dodd-Frank CFTC Agricultural Commodity Definition, 75 Fed. Reg. 65586 (proposed Oct. 26, 2010) (to be codified at 17 C.F.R. pt. 1): The CFTC issued a proposed rule to define "agricultural commodity" under the Commodity Exchange Act (CEA) as amended by Dodd-Frank.	Commodity Markets Council

FINANCIAL SERVICES AGENCIES	
REGULATION/STATUTES/POLICIES	ORGANIZATION/BUSINESS
Dodd-Frank CFTC Agricultural Swaps, 75 Fed. Reg. 59666 (proposed Sept. 28, 2010) (to be codified at 17 C.F.R. pt. 35): The CFTC issued an advance notice of proposed rulemaking to request comment on the appropriate conditions, restrictions or protections to be included in a rule the CFTC must issue under Dodd-Frank governing the trading of agricultural swaps.	Commodity Markets Council
Dodd-Frank CFTC Disruptive Trading Practices, 75 Fed. Reg. 67301 (proposed Nov. 2, 2010) (to be codified at 17 CFR Chapter 1): The CTFC issued an advance notice of proposed rulemaking to request comment on issuing rules necessary to prohibit trading practices deemed disruptive of fair and equitable trading.	Commodity Markets Council
Dodd-Frank Mandatory Clawbacks: Dodd Frank requires companies listed on a U.S. stock exchange to implement and disclose a policy requiring a company to clawback incentive-based compensation paid to current or former executive officers if the company is required to restate its financials due to material non-compliance with financial reporting requirements. The SEC is responsible for enforcing the clawbacks.	American Express Business Roundtable
Dodd-Frank Federal Reserve Board Debit Card Interchange Fees and Routing (proposed Dec. 16, 2010) (to be codified at 12 C.F.R. pt. 235): The Federal Reserve Board issued a proposed rule to establish standards for debit card interchange fees, regulations governing network fees, and prohibitions against network exclusivity arrangements and routing restrictions.	Credit Union National Association Financial Services Roundtable Small Business & Entrepreneurship Council

Table Continued.

FINANCIAL SERVICES AGENCIES	
REGULATION/STATUTES/POLICIES	ORGANIZATION/BUSINESS
Dodd Frank Federal Reserve Board Enhanced Prudential Standards for Large Bank Holding Companies (BHCs) and Nonbank Financial Companies Designated for Consolidated Supervision: The Dodd-Frank Act requires the Federal Reserve Board to establish stricter prudential standards for all BHCs with total consolidated assets of $50 billion or greater and all non-bank financial companies supervised by the Federal Reserve Board. A proposed rule is expected to be issued this spring.	Financial Services Roundtable
Dodd-Frank SEC Facilitating Shareholder Director Nominations ("Proxy Access") 17 C.F.R. §§ 200, 232, 240, 249 (2010): In August 2010, the SEC issued a final rule that requires companies to include board of director nominees by certain shareholders in their proxy materials. Under the rules, shareholders will be eligible to have their nominees included in the proxy materials if they own at least 3 percent of the company's shares continuously for at least the prior three years. However, in October 2010, the SEC announced it would delay implementation of the rule pending the outcome of a court challenge.	American Express Business Roundtable
Dodd-Frank CFTC Prohibition of Market Manipulation, 75 Fed. Reg. 67657 (proposed Nov. 3, 2010) (to be codified at 17 C.F.R. pt. 180): CFTC issued a proposed rule to implement its new anti-manipulation authority. The proposed rules expand and codify the Commission's authority to prohibit manipulation.	Commodity Markets Council

FINANCIAL SERVICES AGENCIES	
REGULATION/STATUTES/POLICIES	ORGANIZATION/BUSINESS
Dodd-Frank SEC Disclosure of Payments by Resource Extraction Issuers, 75 Fed. Reg. 80978 (proposed Dec. 23, 2010) (to be codified at 17 C.F.R. pt. 229, 249): The SEC issued a proposed rule requiring resource extraction issuers to include in an annual report information relating to any payment made by the issuer, or by a subsidiary or another entity controlled by the issuer, to a foreign government or the Federal Government for the purpose of the commercial development of oil, natural gas, or minerals.	Business Roundtable
	ConocoPhillips
Dodd-Frank SEC Mine Safety Disclosure, 75 Fed. Reg. 80374 (proposed Dec. 15, 2010) (to be codified at 17 C.F.R. pt. 229, 239, 249): The SEC issued a proposed rule to outline the way mining companies must disclose certain information about mine safety and health standards to investors.	Business Roundtable
Dodd-Frank SEC Conflict Minerals, 75 Fed. Reg. 80948 (proposed Dec. 23, 2010) (to be codified at 17 C.F.R. pt. 229, 249): The SEC issued a proposed rule that would require any issuer for which conflict minerals are necessary to the functionality or production of a product manufactured, or contracted to be manufactured, by that issuer to disclose in the body of its annual report whether its conflict minerals originated in the Democratic Republic of the Congo or an adjoining country. If so, that issuer would be required to furnish a separate report as an exhibit to its annual report that includes, among other matters, a description of the measures taken by the issuer to exercise due diligence on the source and chain of custody of its conflict minerals.	American Petroleum Institute
	Boeing
	Business Roundtable
	IPC – Association Connecting Electronics Industries
	Manufacturing Jewelers and Suppliers of America
	National Electrical Manufacturers Association

Table Continued.

FINANCIAL SERVICES AGENCIES	
REGULATION/STATUTES/POLICIES	ORGANIZATION/BUSINESS
Dodd-Frank CFTC and SEC Further Definition of "Swap Dealer," "Security-Based Swap Dealer," "Major Swap Participant," "Major Security-Based Swap Participant," and "Eligible Contract Participant", 75 Fed. Reg. 80174 (proposed Dec. 21, 2010) (to be codified at 17 C.F.R. pt. 1, 240): The CFTC and the SEC issued a joint proposed rule that would further define a series of terms related to the security-based swaps market, including "swap dealer," "security-based swap dealer," "major swap participant," "major security-based swap participant" and "eligible contract participant."	American Express
	Business Roundtable
	Commodity Markets Council
	ConocoPhillips
	Edison Electric Institute
Dodd-Frank SEC Implementing Whistleblower Provisions, 75 Fed. Reg. 70488 (proposed Nov. 17, 2010) (to be codified at 17 C.F.R. pt. 240, 249): The SEC issued a proposed rule to implement the whistleblower provisions in Dodd Frank. Under regulations proscribed by the SEC, a whistleblower program will be established, and eligible whistleblowers will receive 10-30% of any fine over $1 million that is a result of original information provided to the SEC that leads to the successful enforcement of a covered action.	American Express
	Boeing
	Business Roundtable

FINANCIAL SERVICES AGENCIES	
REGULATION/STATUTES/POLICIES	ORGANIZATION/BUSINESS
Dodd-Frank Volcker Rule: The Volcker Rule amends the Bank Holding Company Act of 1956 to prohibit banks and other banking entities from engaging in proprietary trading and from sponsoring or investing in private equity or hedge funds. The Volcker Rule also prohibits banks and other banking entities from extending credit to, or engaging in other covered transactions with, private equity or hedge funds that they advise, manage, sponsor, or organize. Any transactions between a banking entity and any such fund that are not prohibited must be entered into on arms-length market terms. Finally, the Volcker Rule tasks the Federal Reserve Board with imposing additional capital and quantitative limits on systemically important nonbank financial companies that engage in proprietary trading or that sponsor or invest in private equity or hedge funds.	Financial Services Roundtable
Federal Credit Union Act Net Worth Restrictions: The Act requires credit unions to have 7% net worth to be considered well-capitalized and 6% net worth to be adequately capitalized.	Credit Union National Association
Secure and Fair Enforcement for Mortgage Licensing Act (SAFE Act) of 2008, Pub. L. No. 110-289: Regulators, specifically at the state level, have broadened the scope of regulated activity to include those who perform administrative and clerical tasks as mortgage loan originators, even if they do not offer or negotiate loan terms for compensation or gain.	Manufactured Housing Institute
President's Working Group Report on Money Market Fund Reform, Release No. IC-29497; File No. 4-619: The SEC is seeking comment on the options discussed in the President's Working Group on Financial Markets' study of possible money market fund reforms. One of the proposals considers moving away from the current stable net asset values (NAVs) to a floating NAV.	Boeing

Table Continued.

FINANCIAL SERVICES AGENCIES	
REGULATION/STATUTES/POLICIES	ORGANIZATION/BUSINESS
Sarbanes-Oxley Act (SOX), Pub. L. No. 107-204, § 404(b), 116 Stat. 745 (2002): SOX Section 404(b) requires public companies to conduct a review of internal controls over financial reporting and include an external auditor attestation report of those controls in their annual filings.	Biotechnology Industry Organization
Joint Agency Red Flags Rule, 12 C.F.R. § 41 (2007): In 2007, pursuant to the Fair and Accurate Credit Transactions Act of 2003, the OCC, Board, FDIC, OTS, NCUA and FTC jointly issued rules that require financial institutions and creditors to develop and implement identify theft programs. The programs must include identification, detection and response to patterns, practices, or specific activities that could indicate identity theft	American Land Title Association National Automobile Dealers Association
FTC and Federal Reserve Board Fair Credit Reporting Risk-Based Pricing Rule, 16 C.F.R. §§640, 698 (2010): Pursuant to the Fair and Accurate Credit Transaction Act of 2003, the FTC and Federal Reserve Board issued a rule that generally requires a creditor to provide a risk-based pricing notice to a consumer when the creditor uses a consumer report to grant or extend credit to the consumer on material terms that are materially less favorable than the most favorable terms available to a substantial proportion of consumers from or through that creditor.	National Automobile Dealers Association

DEPARTMENT OF LABOR/LABOR ISSUES	
REGULATION/STATUTES/POLICIES	ORGANIZATION/BUSINESS
Administration "High Road" Government Contracting Policy: The February 2010 Annual Report of the White House Task Force on the Middle Class announced it is exploring a government contacting policy that would take into account the records of the firms who receive government contracts and the quality of the jobs they create.	Associated Builders and Contractors, Inc.
	Associated General Contractors
	Small Business & Entrepreneurship Council
Administration Use of Project Labor Agreements for Federal Construction Projects (E.O. 13502) and 48 C.F.R. § 536.271 (2010): On February 13, 2009, President Obama issued an Executive Order to encourage the use of project labor agreements for large-scale federal construction projects. In April 2010, the Department of Defense, General Services Administration, and National Aeronautics and Space Administration issued a final rule implementing the Executive Order.	Associated Builders and
	Associated General Contractors
	Construction Industry Round Table
	Small Business & Entrepreneurship Council
DOL's Lack of Clarity in Job Duties used for Wage Determinations under the Davis-Bacon Act: Currently, DOL provides wage determination lists for several different classifications of workers, but only limited information is provided about the job duties or union work rules that correspond to those classifications.	Associated Builders and Contractors, Inc.
DOL Persuader Agreements: Employer and Labor Relations Consultant Reporting Under the Labor-Management Reporting and Disclosure Act (LMRDA) (Potential): In the fall of 2010, the Office of Labor Management Standards announced they plan to propose a rule to reinterpret section 203(c) of the LMRDA to narrow the scope of the advice exemption.	Associated Builders and Contractors, Inc.

Table Continued.

DEPARTMENT OF LABOR/LABOR ISSUES	
REGULATION/STATUTES/POLICIES	ORGANIZATION/BUSINESS
DOL Right to Know under the Fair Labor Standards Act (FLSA) (Potential): In the fall of 2010, the Wage and Hour Division (WHD) announced they are considering a proposed rule that would required covered employers to notify their employees of their rights under the FLSA and to provide information about hours worked and wage computation. The proposal is expected to be issued in April 2011.	American Bakers Association Associated Builders and National Federation of Independent Business
DOL Wage Rates Under the Davis-Bacon Act: The Wage and Hour Division (WHD) sets "prevailing wages" based on wages paid to various laborers and mechanics employed on construction projects.	Associated Builders and Contractors, Inc.
Employee Benefits Security Administration (EBSA) Definition of the Term "Fiduciary" 75 Fed. Reg. 2142 (proposed Oct. 22, 2010): The EBSA issued a proposed rule to expand the definition of "fiduciary" under the Employee Retirement Income Security Act (ERISA).	Financial Services Forum (note this concern may not reflect the entire membership of the Forum)
NLRB Governing Notification of Employee Rights under the National Labor Relations Act (NLRA), 75 Fed. Reg. 80420 (proposed Dec. 22, 2010) (to be codified to 29 C.F.R. pt. 104): The NLRB issued a proposed rule that would require employers, including labor organizations, to post notices informing their employees of their rights under the NLRA.	Associated Builders and Contractors, Inc. Forging Industry Association Motor and Equipment National Council of Textile National Restaurant Association Non-Ferrous Founders' Society Textile Rental Services Association
OHSA Backing Operations (Potential): In the fall of 2010, OSHA announced it is considering proposing a rule to regulate the backing operations of construction equipment.	Associated General Contractors
OSHA Building Inspectors Partnership (pilot program): In May 2010, OSHA announced it is launching a pilot program to partner with local building inspectors in select American cities to monitor working conditions.	Associated General Contractors

DEPARTMENT OF LABOR/LABOR ISSUES	
REGULATION/STATUTES/POLICIES	ORGANIZATION/BUSINESS
OSHA Combustible Dust, 74 Fed. Reg. 54334 (proposed Oct. 21, 2009) (to be codified at 29 C.F.R. pt. 1910): OSHA issued an advanced notice of proposed rulemaking to develop a proposed standard for combustible dust management. OHSA has determined combustible dust to include "all combustible particulate solids of any size, shape, or chemical composition that could present a fire or deflagration hazard when suspended in air or other oxidizing medium."	American Forest and Paper American Iron and Steel Institute American Wire Producers APA - The Engineered Wood Kitchen Cabinet Manufacturers National Lumber & Building National Oilseed Processors Non-Ferrous Founders' Society Society of Plastics Industry
OSHA Consultation Agreements: Proposed Changes to Consultation Procedures, 75 Fed. Reg. 54064 (proposed Sept. 3, 2010) (to be codified at 29 C.F.R. pt. 1908): OSHA issued a proposed rule to clarify the Assistant Secretary's ability to identify sites to be inspected, regardless of their Safety and Health Achievement and Recognition Programs (SHARP) status. The proposal also permits OSHA compliance officers to proceed with enforcement visits due to referrals from sites undergoing consultation visits or sites that have attained SHARP status. Finally, the proposal limits the deletion period from OSHA's programmed inspection schedule for those employers that participate in the SHARP program.	American Coatings Association American Iron and Steel Institute Associated General Contractors International Bottled Water Metal Treating Institute Motor and Equipment National Association of National Federation of Independent Society of Plastics Industry Textile Rental Services Association
OSHA Cranes and Derricks in Construction, 29 C.F.R. § 1926 (2010): OSHA issued a final rule to update and specify industry work practices to help ensure employee safety during the use of cranes and derrick in construction projects. The rule took effect on November 8, 2010.	Association of Equipment Manufacturers

Table Continued.

DEPARTMENT OF LABOR/LABOR ISSUES	
REGULATION/STATUTES/POLICIES	ORGANIZATION/BUSINESS
OSHA Injury & Illness Prevention Program ("I2P2") 75 Fed. Reg. 23637 (proposed May 4, 2010) (to be codified at C.F.R. pt. 1910): OSHA announced it was conducting stakeholder meetings to develop a proposed rule to implement an Injury and Illness Prevention Program. The proposed rule is expected to be issued this spring, and it is likely to address how to plan, implement, evaluate, and improve processes and activities that protect employee safety and health.	American Coatings Association
	American Iron and Steel Institute
	Associated Builders and Contractors, Inc.
	Associated General Contractors
	Metal Treating Institute
	Motor and Equipment Manufacturers Association
	National Association of Manufacturers
	National Federation of Independent Business
	National Lumber & Building Material Dealers Association
	National Oilseed Processors Association
	Small Business & Entrepreneurship Council
	Society of Plastics Industry
	Textile Rental Services Association
OSHA Interpretation of Provisions for Feasible Administrative or Engineering Controls of Occupational Noise 75 Fed. Reg. 64216 (proposed Oct. 19, 2010) (to be codified at 29 C.F.R. pt. 1910, 1926): OSHA issued a proposed interpretation of the term "feasible administrative or engineering controls" to clarify that the term "feasible" means capable of being done. On January 19th, 2011, OSHA announced it was withdrawing its proposed interpretation.	American Coatings Association
	American Coke and Coal Chemicals Institute
	American Forest and Paper Association
	American Iron and Steel Institute
	APA - The Engineered Wood Association
	Associated Builders and Contractors, Inc.
	Associated General Contractors
	Association of Equipment Manufacturers
	Boeing

DEPARTMENT OF LABOR/LABOR ISSUES	
REGULATION/STATUTES/POLICIES	ORGANIZATION/BUSINESS
	Conoco-Phillips, Inc
	Forging Industry Association
	International Bottled Water Association
	Kitchen Cabinet Manufacturers Association
	Metal Treating Institute
	Motor and Equipment Manufacturers Association
	National Association of Manufacturers
	National Concrete Masonry Association
	National Council of Textile Organizations
	National Federation of Independent Business
	National Lumber & Building Material Dealers Association
	National Oilseed Processors Association
	National Tooling and Machining Association
	Non-Ferrous Founders' Society
	Precision Machined Products Association
	Precision Metalforming Association
	Roaring Springs Water
	Small Business & Entrepreneurship Council
	Society of Plastics Industry
	Textile Rental Services Association
	Window & Door Manufacturers Association

Table Continued.

DEPARTMENT OF LABOR/LABOR ISSUES	
REGULATION/STATUTES/POLICIES	ORGANIZATION/BUSINESS
OSHA Lockout Procedure Guidance: In 2008, OSHA issued a compliance directive to make clear that efforts to label die or tool changes as "routine, repetitive and integral to the production operation" and therefore not subject to lockout would be rejected.	National Tooling and Machining Association
	Precision Machined Products Association
	Precision Metalforming Association
OSHA Occupational Exposure to Crystalline Silica (Potential): In the fall of 2010, OSHA announced it intends to pursue a new comprehensive standard for crystalline silica to require provisions for methods of compliance, exposure monitoring, worker training, and medical surveillance. A proposal is expected to be issued in February 2011.	Associated General Contractors
	Interlocking Concrete Pavement Institute
	National Concrete Masonry Association
OSHA Occupational Injury and Illness Recording and Reporting Requirements, 75 Fed. Reg. 4728 (proposed Jan. 29, 2010) (to be codified at 29 C.F.R. pt. 1904): OSHA issued a proposed rule to add a column to the OSHA 300 Log that would require employers to record work-related musculoskeletal disorders (MSD). On January 25, 2011, OSHA announced it was temporarily withdrawing its proposed rule to seek further input from small business.	American Coke and Coal Chemicals Institute
	American Iron and Steel Institute
	Associated Builders and Contractors, Inc.
	Associated General Contractors
	Automotive Aftermarket Industry Association
	Metal Treating Institute
	National Federation of Independent Business
	National Oilseed Processors Association
	Non-Ferrous Founders' Society
	Society of Chemical Manufacturers and Affiliates
	Society of Plastics Industry

DEPARTMENT OF LABOR/LABOR ISSUES	
REGULATION/STATUTES/POLICIES	ORGANIZATION/BUSINESS
OSHA Permissible Exposure Limit (PEL): In August 2010, OSHA announced it plans to conduct a comprehensive review of chemicals that should be subject to PELs.	American Iron and Steel Institute Metal Treating Institute
OSHA Policy Change to Penalty Structure:OSHA is currently implementing multiple changes to its administrative penalty calculation system that will impact final penalties issued to employers for OSHA violations.	Associated General Contractors
OSHA Safety Signs: Current safety sign regulations are based on outdated standards.	National Electrical Manufacturers Association
OSHA Severe Violator Enforcement **Program (SVEP)**:In June 2010, OSHA established enforcement policies and procedures for the SVEP toreplace OSHA's Enhanced Enforcement Program (EEP).	Non-Ferrous Founders' Society

DEPARTMENT OF TRANSPORTATION	
REGULATION/STATUTES/POLICIES	ORGANIZATION/BUSINESS
Hours of Service 75 Fed. Reg. 82170 (proposed Dec. 29, 2010) (to be codified at 49 C.F.R. pt. 385, 386, 390, 395):The Hours-of-Service regulations put limits in place for when and how long commercial motor vehicle (CMV) drivers may drive.	American Bakers Association Grocery Manufacturers Association Metal Treating Institute National Association of Manufacturers
DOT Proposed Rule on Transportation of Lithium Batteries 75 Fed. Reg. 1302 (proposed Jan. 11, 2010) (to be codified at 49 C.F.R. pt. 172, 173, 175): Unless excepted by specific provisions, Lithium batteries must be approved for commercial transportation by PHMSA's Associate Administrator for Hazardous Materials Safety.	Air Transport Association CTIA-The Wireless Association National Association of Manufacturers Metal Treating Institute National Electric Manufacturers Association

Table Continued.

DEPARTMENT OF TRANSPORTATION	
REGULATION/STATUTES/POLICIES	ORGANIZATION/BUSINESS
Cargo Capacity Labeling Rule or Part 571.110: Tire selection and rims and motor home/recreation vehicle trailer load carrying capacity information for motor vehicles with a GVWR of 4,536 kilograms (10,000 pounds) or less 49 C.R.F. §571.110 (2003):This standard specifies requirements for tire selection to prevent tire overloading and for motor home/recreation vehicle trailer load carrying capacity information.	National Automobile Dealers Association
FAA: Flightcrew Member Duty and Rest Requirements, 75 Fed. Reg. 63424 (proposed Oct. 15, 2010) (to be codified at 14 C.F.R. pt. 117, 121):Imposes duty-time limitations and rest requirements for Part 121 carriers. The proposal would limit the daily flight-duty period to 13 hours, which could slide to nine hours at night (depending on takeoff time and number of segments scheduled). Current rules allow for a 16-hour duty period between rest periods. The proposed rule defines "flight duty" as the period of time when a pilot reports for duty with the intention of flying an aircraft, operating a simulator or operating a flight-training device. A pilot's entire duty period can include both "flight duty" and other tasks that do not involve flight time, such as record keeping and ground training.	Air Transport Association
Hazardous Materials Transportation Special Permit Program,76 Fed. Reg. 454 (proposed Jan. 5, 2011) (to be codified at 49 C.F.R. pt. 105, 106, 171):The Pipeline and Hazardous Materials Safety Administration is revising its procedures for applying for a special permit to require an applicant to provide sufficient information about its operations to enable the agency to evaluate the applicant's fitness and the safety impact of operations that would be authorized in the special permit. In addition, PHMSA is providing an on-line application option.	Agricultural Retailers Association Motor and Equipment Manufacturers Association

DEPARTMENT OF TRANSPORTATION	
REGULATION/STATUTES/POLICIES	ORGANIZATION/BUSINESS
Hours of Service; Limited Exemption for the Distribution of Anhydrous Ammonia in Agricultural Operations, 75 Fed. Reg. 40765 (proposed July 14, 2010) (to be codified at 49 C.F.R. pt. 395): This proposalgrants a 2-year, limited exemption from the Federal hours-of-service regulations for the transportation of anhydrous ammonia from any distribution point to a local farm retailer or to the ultimate consumer, and from a local farm retailer to the ultimate consumer, as long as the transportation takes place within a 100 air-mile radius of the retail or wholesale distribution point. This exemption would extend the agricultural operations exemption established by section 345 of the National Highway System Designation Act of 1995, as amended, by the sections 4115 and 4130 of the Safe, Accountable, Flexible, Efficient Transportation Equity: A Legacy for Users (SAFETEA-LU) to certain drivers and motor carriers engaged in the distribution of anhydrous ammonia during the planting and harvesting seasons, as defined by the States in which the carriers and drivers operate.	Agricultural Retailers Association

MISCELLANEOUS

CONSUMER PRODUCT SAFETY COMMISSION	
REGULATION/STATUTES/POLICIES	ORGANIZATION/BUSINESS
Consumer Product Safety Improvement Act of 2008, Pub. L. No. 110-314: specifying lead levels in children's products	Manufacturing Jewelers & Suppliers of America
	Motorcycle Industry Council
	National Council of Textile Organizations
Testing and Labeling Pertaining to Product Certification, 75 Fed. Reg. 28336 (proposed May 20, 2010) (to be codified at16 C.F.R. pt. 1107): On May 20, 2010, CPSC proposed a rule that would establish requirements for a reasonable testing program and for compliance and continuing testing for children's products.	International Sleep Products Association

DEPARTMENT OF AGRICULTURE	
REGULATION/STATUTES/POLICIES	ORGANIZATION/BUSINESS
"Buy America" Policy	Bumble Bee Foods, LLC
Implementation of Regulations Required Under Title XI of the Food, Conservation and Energy Act of 2008 (Proposed) 75 Fed. Reg. 44163 (proposed July 28, 2010) (to be codified at 9 C.F.R. pt. 201): The Department of Agriculture (USDA), Grain Inspection, Packers and Stockyards Administration (GIPSA) is proposing to add several new sections to the regulations under the Packers and Stockyards Act, 1921, as amended and supplemented (PS Act).	American Meat Institute
Plant Protection Act (PPA)of 2000 as part of the Agricultural Risk Protection Act: The PPA consolidates all or part of 10 existing USDA plant health laws into one comprehensive law, including the authority to regulate plants, plant products, certain biological control organisms, noxious weeds, and plant pests.	Biotechnology Industry Organization
U.S. Sugar Program	American Bakers Association

DEPARTMENT OF ENERGY	
REGULATION/STATUTES/POLICIES	ORGANIZATION/BUSINESS
National Environmental Policy Act Implementing Procedures (Proposed) 76 Fed. Reg. 214 (proposed Jan. 3, 2011) (to be codified at 10 C.F.R. pt. 1021): The U.S. Department of Energy proposes to amend its existing regulations governing compliance with the National Environmental Policy Act (NEPA). The majority of the changes are proposed for the categorical exclusions provisions contained in its NEPA Implementing Procedures, with a small number of related changes proposed for other provisions.	Plumbing Manufacturers Institute

DEPARTMENT OF HEALTH AND HUMAN SERVICES	
REGULATION/STATUTES/POLICIES	ORGANIZATION/BUSINESS
Accounting of Disclosures: Health Information Technology for Economic and Clinical Health (HITECH) Act	National Association of Chain Drug Stores
Centers for Medicare and Medicaid (CMS): Health IT Interim Final Rule	American Express
	Business Roundtable
Centers for Medicare and Medicaid (CMS): Medicare Provider Enrollment, Chain and Ownership System	National Association of Chain Drug Stores
Centers for Medicare and Medicaid (CMS): Durable Medical Equipment and Supplies Competitive Bidding	National Association of Chain Drug Stores
Centers for Medicare and Medicaid (CMS): Medicare/Medicaid Recovery Audit Contractor (RAC) Program	American Hospital Association
Centers for Medicare and Medicaid (CMS): Clinical Laboratory Signature on Requisition	American Hospital Association

Table Continued.

DEPARTMENT OF HEALTH AND HUMAN SERVICES	
REGULATION/STATUTES/POLICIES	ORGANIZATION/BUSINESS
Centers for Medicare and Medicaid (CMS): Retiree Drug Subsidy under Patient Protection and Affordable Care Act (PPACA)	American Express
	Business Roundtable
The Civil Money Penalty Law	American Hospital Association
Employer Mandate: Patient Protection and Affordable Care Act (PPACA)	American Express
	Business Roundtable
	Small Business & Entrepreneurship Council
The Ethics in Patient Referrals Act (The Stark Law): administered jointly with the Department of Justice	American Hospital Association
Grandfathering Rule: Patient Protection and Affordable Care Act (PPACA)	American Express
	Business Roundtable
	Small Business & Entrepreneurship Council
Medical Loss Ratio Rule: Patient Protection and Affordable Care Act (PPACA)	American Express
	Business Roundtable
	Small Business & Entrepreneurship Council
Regulation Abolishing "Mini-Medical" Plans: Patient Protection and Affordable Care Act (PPACA)	American Express
	Business Roundtable
	Small Business & Entrepreneurship Council

DEPARTMENT OF HOMELAND SECURITY	
REGULATION/STATUTES/POLICIES	ORGANIZATION/BUSINESS
Aircraft Repair Station Security, 74 Fed. Reg. 59874) (proposed Nov. 18, 2009) (to be codified at 49 C.F.R. pts. 1520 and 1554): Transportation Security Administration (TSA) is proposing a rule to codify the scope of its existing inspection program and to require regulated parties to allow TSA and Department of Homeland Security (DHS) officials to enter, inspect, and test property, facilities, and records relevant to repair stations. The proposed regulations also provide procedures for TSA to notify repair stations of any deficiencies in their security programs, and to determine whether a particular repair station presents an immediate risk to security.	Aircraft Owners and Pilots Association
Maryland Three Airports: Enhanced Security Procedures at Certain Airports in the Washington, D.C., Area, 49 C.F.R. § 1562: TSA published an interim final rule (IFR) on February 10, 2005 (70 FR 7150), codified and transferred responsibility from the Federal Aviation Administration (FAA) to TSA for ground security requirements and procedures at three Maryland airports that are located within the Washington, DC, Metropolitan Area Flight Restricted Zone (Maryland Three Airports), and for individuals operating aircraft to or from these three airports.	Aircraft Owners and Pilots Association

FEDERAL COMMUNICATIONS COMMISSION	
REGULATION/STATTES/POLICIES	ORGANIZATION/BUSINESS
Empowering Consumers to Avoid Bill Shock Consumer Information and Disclosure(FCC 10-180):The Federal Communications Commission proposes rules that would require mobile service providers to provide usage alerts and information that will assist consumers in avoiding unexpected charges on their bills.	CTIA--The Wireless Association
FFC Form 355: television broadcasters must prepare each calendar quarter a new disclosure form and to place the form in their public inspection files.	National Association of Broadcasters
National Broadband Plan:As directed by Congress, the FCC developed a plan to concerning access to broadband capability.	Edison Electric Institute

FEDERAL RAILROAD ADMINISTRATION	
REGULATION/STATUTES/POLICIES	ORGANIZATION/BUSINESS
Railroad Safety Enhancement Act of 2008, Pub. L. No. 110-432:Rail Safety Improvement Act of 2008 - (Sec. 3) Authorizes appropriations for FY2009-FY2013 for: (1) railroad safety; (2) the purchase of Gage Restraint Measurement System vehicles and track geometry vehicles or other comparable technology to assess track safety; and (3) construction of the Facility for Underground Rail Station and Tunnel at the Transportation Technology Center, Inc., in Pueblo, Colorado.	Association of American Railroads

INTERNAL REVENUE SERVICE	
REGULATION/STATUTES/POLICIES	ORGANIZATION/BUSINESS
1099 Reporting Mandate: Patient Protection and Affordable Care Act (PPACA)	American Bakers Association
	American Express
	Associated Builders and Contractors
	Business Roundtable
	Manufacturing Jewelers & Suppliers of America
	National Community Pharmacists Association
	Small Business & Entrepreneurship Council
Cadillac Tax: Patient Protection and Affordable Care Act (PPACA)	American Express
	Business Roundtable
3% Withholding Mandate: Tax Increase Prevention and Reconciliation Act of 2005	Aerospace Industries Association
	Associated Builders and Contractors
	Computing Technology Industry Association
	Government Withholding Relief Coalition
	National Asphalt Pavement Association
	Small Business & Entrepreneurship Council
Interpretation of Section 199 of the Internal Revenue Code	Institute of Scrap Recycling Industries
Deduction and Capitalization of Expenditures Related to Tangible Property	Textile Rental Services Association

APPENDIX II. ENVIRONMENTAL REGULATORY TIMELINE FOR COAL UNITS

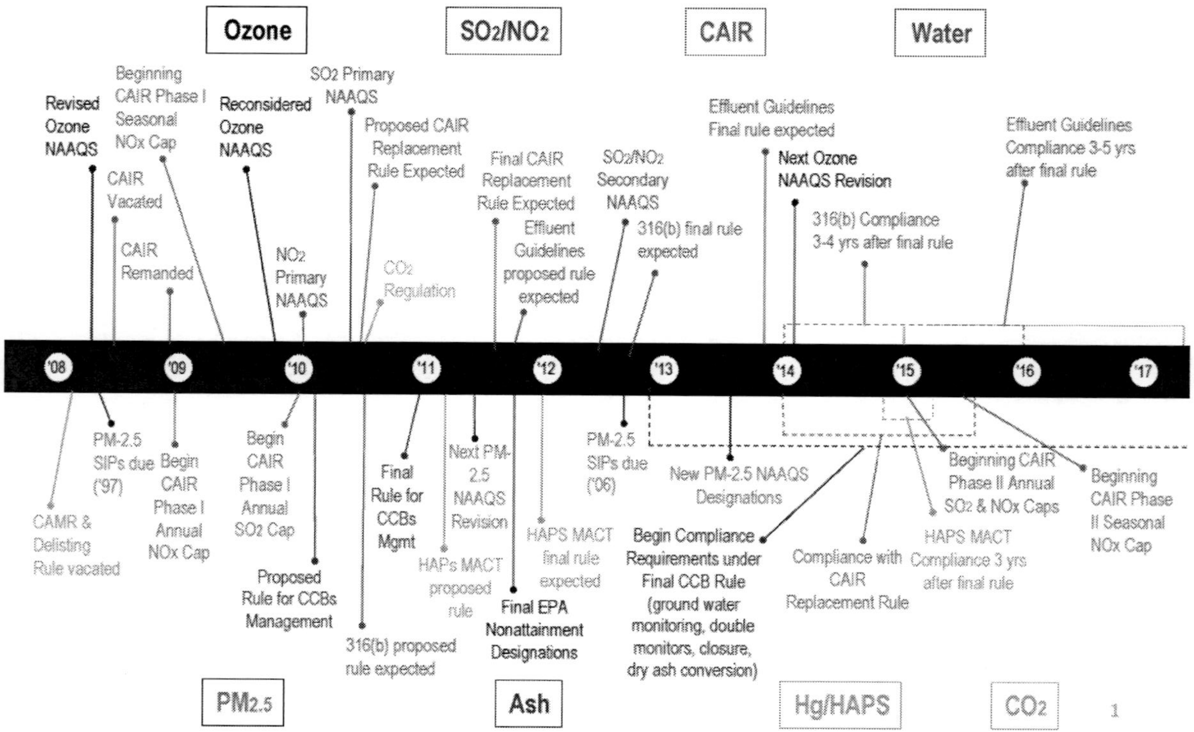

End Notes

[1] Press Release, U.S. Department of Labor Bureau of Labor Statistics, The Employment Situation – December 2010 (Feb. 4, 2011).

[2] Ron Scherer, *Unemployment Rate Dives, But Few New Jobs Created. How Can That Be?* CHRISTIAN SCIENCE MONITOR, Feb. 4, 2011.

[3] Alister Bull & Caren Bohan, *Obama Pledges Cooperation in Outreach to Business*, REUTERS, Oct. 4, 2010, http://www.reuters.com/article/2010/10/04/us-obama-business-idUSTRE6935SS20101004?feedType=RSS&feedName=everything&virtualBrandChannel =11563.

[4] Press Release, U.S. Department of Labor Bureau of Labor Statistics, The Employment Situation – January 2011 (Feb. 4, 2011).

[5] *Sizing Up the 2007-2009 Recession: Comparing Two Key Labor Market Indicators with Earlier Downturns*, ISSUES IN LAB. STAT. (U.S. DOL – BLS), Dec. 2010, at 2.

[6] *Ranks of Those Unemployed for a Year or More Up Sharply*, ISSUES IN LAB. STAT. (U.S. DOL – BLS), Oct. 2010, at 1.

[7] R. HEDERMAN & J. SHERK, HERITAGE EMPLOYMENT REPORT: LITTLE CAUSE FOR THANKSGIVING IN NOVEMBER JOBS REPORT, THE HERITAGE FOUNDATION 1 (2010).

[8] Press Release, U.S. Department of Labor Bureau of Labor Statistics, The Employment Situation – December 2010, (Jan. 7, 2011).

[9] Sam Sanders, *Black Teenage Males Crushed By Unemployment*, NPR, Jan. 10, 2010, available at http://www.npr.org/templates/story/story.php?storyId=122367407.

[10] *Id.*

[11] BUREAU OF LABOR STATISTICS, LABOR FORCE STATISTICS FROM THE CURRENT POPULATION SURVEY TEN YEAR UNEMPLOYMENT RATE (2011), http://data.bls.gov/pdq /SurveyOutputServlet?data_tool=latest_numbers&series_id=LNS14000000.

[12] Lydia Saad, *In U.S., Jobs Are Top Problem, While New High Cite Deficit*, GALLUP Jan. 13, 2011, http:// www.gallup.com/poll/145571/jobs-top-problem-new-high-cite-deficit.aspx.

[13] *Importance of Issues Voter Concern About Economy Hits Highest Level in Over Two Years*, RASMUSSEN REPORTS, Jan. 4, 2011, http://www.rasmussenreports.com/public_content/ politics/mood_ of_america/ importance_ofjssues.

[14] Press Release, U.S. Department of Labor Bureau of Labor Statistics, Regional and State Employment and Unemployment – December 2010 (Jan. 25, 2010).

[15] *Id.*

[16] *An Occupational Analysis of Industries with the Most Job Losses*, OCCUPATIONAL EMPLOYMENT STATISTICS HIGHLIGHTS (U.S. DOL – BLS), Nov. 2009, at 1-2.

[17] *Recession Leads to Lackluster Employment in the Trucking Industry*, ISSUES IN LABOR STATISTICS (U.S. DOL – BLS), Feb. 2010.

[18] U.S. DEPARTMENT OF LABOR, BUREAU OF LABOR STATISTICS, CURRENT EMPLOYMENT STATISTICS HIGHLIGHTS NOVEMBER 2010, (Dec. 2010), http://www.bls.gov/ces/highlights112010.pdf.

[19] Press Release, U.S. Department of Labor Bureau of Labor Statistics, Employment Projections 2008-18 (Dec. 10, 2009).

[20] *Id.*

21 U.S. DEPARTMENT OF LABOR, BUREAU OF LABOR STATISTICS, CURRENT EMPLOYMENT STATISTICS HIGHLIGHTS NOVEMBER 2010, (Dec. 2010), http://www.bls.gov/ces/highlights112010.pdf.

22 *Id.*

23 Press Release, U.S. Department of Labor Bureau of Labor Statistics, The Employment Situation – December 2010 (Jan. 7, 2011).

24 Veronique de Rugy, *Has Government Grown Since the Recession Started?,* NATIONAL REVIEW, Dec. 28, 2010, http://www.nationalreview.com/corner/255951/has-government-grown-recession-startedveronique-de-rugy.

25 WILLIAM C. DUNKELBERG & HOLLY WADE, NFIB SMALL BUSINESS ECONOMIC TRENDS, 1-3 (Dec. 2010).

26 *Id.*

27 *Id.*

28 Letter from Ivan G. Seidenberg, Chairman, Business Roundtable to the Hon. Peter Orszag (June 21, 2010) available at http://businessroundtable.org/news-center/business-roundtable-letter-to-the-whitehouse-on-policy-burdens-inhibi/.

29 Alister Bull & Caren Bohan, *Obama Pledges Cooperation in Outreach to Business*, REUTERS, Oct. 4, 2010, http://www.reuters.com/article/2010/10/04/us-obama-business-idUSTRE6935SS20101004?feedType=RSS&feedName=everything&virtualBrandChannel=11563.

30 *Obama Business Outreach Includes P&G, Wal-Mart*, DAYTON BUSINESS JOURNAL, Dec. 1, 2010, http://www.bizjournals.com/dayton/news/2010/12/01/obama-biz-outreach-includes-pg-walmart.html.

31 Matt Spetalnick, *Obama to Host CEO Summit Wednesday in Outreach to Business*, MSNBC, Dec. 12, 2010, http://www.msnbc.msn.com/id/40620171/ns/business-us_business/.

32 *Id.*

33 President Barack Obama, Address at Signing of the Small Business Jobs Act (Sept. 27, 2010).

34 *Assessing the Regulatory and Administrative Burdens on America's Small Businesses: Hearing Before the S. Comm. on Small Business and* Entrepreneurship, 111th Cong. (2010) (testimony of Dr. Winslow Sargeant).

35 U.S. Small Business Administration Frequently Asked Questions, Advocacy Small Business Statistics and Research, http://web.sba.gov/faqs/faqIndexAll.cfm?areaid=24 (last visited Feb. 3, 2011).

36 *Assessing the Regulatory and Administrative Burdens on America's Small Businesses: Hearing Before the S. Comm. on Small Business and* Entrepreneurship, 111th Cong. (2010) (testimony of Dr. Winslow Sargeant).

37 NICOLE V. CRAIN & W. MARK CRAIN, THE IMPACT OF REGULATORY COSTS ON SMALL FIRMS, SBA OFFICE OF ADVOCACY 6 (2010).

38 *Id.* at 51.

39 CLYDE WAYNE CREWS, JR., TEN THOUSAND COMMANDMENTS: AN ANNUAL SNAPSHOT OF THE FEDERAL REGULATORY STATE 1 (2010).

40 CRAIN & CRAIN at 51.

41 *Id.* at 8.

42 *Id.*

43 *Id.* at 6.

44 Letter from Phillip D. Brady, President, Nat'l Auto. Dealers Assoc., to Darrell Issa, Chairman, Comm. on Oversight & Gov't Reform, (Jan. 5, 2011) (on file with author).

[45] THE REGULATORY MAZE, NADA'S ANNUAL UPDATE ON FEDERAL REGULATIONS (2010).

[46] Letter from Phillip D. Brady, President, Nat'l Auto. Dealers Assoc., to Darrell Issa, Chairman, Comm. on Oversight & Gov't Reform, (Jan. 5, 2011) (on file with author).

[47] CRAIN & CRAIN at 51.

[48] *Id.* at 56.

[49] Letter from Jay Timmons, Nat'l Ass'n of Manufacturers, to Darrell Issa, Chairman, Comm. on Oversight & Gov't Reform (Jan. 7, 2011) (on file with author).

[50] Bureau of Labor Statistics, Establishment Data State and Area Employment (Oct. 2010).

[51] Letter from Richard Williams, Ph.D., Dir. of Policy Research, Mercatus Ctr, to Darrell Issa, Chairman, Comm. on Oversight & Gov't Reform (Jan. 5, 2011) (on file with author).

[52] Brendan Case, *Texans Have It Good, Dallas Fed Chief Says*, DALLAS MORNING NEWS, July 30, 2010, at D01.

[53] *Id.*

[54] Telecom Notes, Communication Daily (Mar. 31, 2010).

[55] Vicki Smith, *EPA Accused of 'Assault on Mining Industry' After Revoking Permit for Mountaintop Mine*, CNSNEWS, Jan. 14, 2011, http://www.cnsnews.com/news/article/epa-accused-assault-miningindustry-afte.

[56] *Id.*

[57] Elise Echeverri-Carroll & Sofia G. Ayala, *Regulation and American Business*, HOOVER INSTITUTION POLICY REVIEW NO. 155 (2009).

[58] *Id.*

[59] Alana Semuels, *Losses of Factory Jobs in California Blamed on Regulation*, L.A. TIMES, June 23, 2009.

[60] Ross C. DeVol, et. al, *Manufacturing 2.0: A More Prosperous California*, THE MILKEN INSTITUTE, (2009).

[61] Letter from Richard Williams, Ph.D., Dir. of Policy Research, Mercatus Ctr., to Darrell Issa, Chairman, Comm. on Oversight & Gov't Reform (Jan. 5, 2011) (on file with author).

[62] *Id.*

[63] Letter from Stephen E. Sandherr, CEO, Associated Gen. Contractors of America, to Darrell Issa, Ranking Member, Comm. on Oversight & Gov't Reform (Dec. 30, 2010) (on file with the author).

[64] *Id.*

[65] Letter from Sean Thurman, Senior Manager, Associated Builders and Contractors, Inc., to Darrell Issa, Chairman, Comm. on Oversight & Gov't Reform, (Jan. 7, 2011) (on file with author).

[66] CURTIS W. COPELAND, CONGRESSIONAL RESEARCH SERVICE, FEDERAL RULEMAKING: THE ROLE OF THE OFFICE OF INFORMATION AND REGULATORY AFFAIRS 2 (2009).

[67] Exec. Order No. 12,291, 46 Fed. Reg. 13,193 (Feb. 19, 1981).

[68] Exec. Order No. 12,291, 46 Fed. Reg. 13,193 (Feb. 19, 1981).

[69] Copeland at 4.

[70] Exec. Order No. 12,498, 50 Fed. Reg. 1,036 (Jan. 8, 1985).

[71] Copeland at 4.

[72] CURTIS W. COPELAND, CONGRESSIONAL RESEARCH SERVICE, *FEDERAL RULEMAKING: THE ROLE OF THE OFFICE OF INFORMATION AND REGULATORY AFFAIRS* 2 (2009).

[73] Exec. Order No. 12,866, 58 Fed. Reg. 51,735 (Oct. 4, 1993).

[74] *Id.*
[75] *Id.*
[76] Exec. Order No. 12,866, 58 Fed. Reg. 51,735 (Oct. 4, 1993).
[77] Barack Obama, Op-Ed., *Toward a 21st-Century Regulatory System*, WALL ST. J., Jan. 18, 2011.
[78] Exec. Order No. 13,563, 76 Fed. Reg. 3,821 (Jan. 18, 2011).
[79] Editorial, *Obama's Rule-Making Loophole*, WALL ST. J, Jan. 21, 2011.
[80] SUSAN DUDLEY, THE GEORGE WASHINGTON UNIVERSITY REGULATORY STUDIES CENTER, PRESIDENT OBAMA'S EXECUTIVE ORDER: IMPROVING REGULATION AND REGULATORY REVIEW (2011), http://www.regulatorystudies.gwu.edu/images/commentary/20110118_reg_eo.pdf.
[81] *Id.*
[82] Letter from Jennifer Joy Wilson, Vice President, Nat'l Stone, Sand and Gravel Ass'n to Darrell Issa, Chairman, Comm. on Oversight & Gov't Reform (Jan. 7, 2011) (on file with author).
[83] John Judis, *The Quiet Revolution*, THE NEW REPUBLIC, Feb. 1, 2010 (available at: http://www.tnr.com/article/politics/the-quiet-revolution?page=0,1).
[84] *Id.*
[85] Electricity Prices for Industry, http://www.eia.doe.gov/emeu/international/elecprii.html.
[86] U.S. ENERGY INFORMATION ADMINISTRATION, ANNUAL ENERGY REVIEW 2009 5 (2010), *available at* http://www.eia.doe.gov/emeu/aer/pdf/pages/sec1_5.pdf.
[87] U.S. ENERGY INFORMATION ADMINISTRATION, ELECTRIC POWER ANNUAL 2009 2 (2011), *available at* http://www.eia.gov/cneaf/electricity/epa/epa.pdf.
[88] For additional discussion of EPA regulations see section VII.C.1,2,&3.
[89] Letter from Donna Harman, President & CEO, American Forest & Paper Association, to Darrell Issa, Chairman, Comm. on Oversight & Gov't Reform 2 (Jan. 10, 2011) (on file with author).
[90] Letter from William Kovacs, Vice President, U.S. Chamber of Commerce to Darrell Issa, Ranking Member, Comm. on Oversight & Gov't Reform (Dec. 29, 2010).
[91] Letter from Karen Bennett, Vice President, Environmental Affairs, National Mining Association to Darrell Issa, Chairman, Comm. on Oversight & Gov't Reform, Attachment 2, 4 (Jan. 6, 2011) (on file with author).
[92] *Id.*
[93] DAN EGGERS ET AL, GROWTH FROM SUBTRACTION: IMPACT OF EPA RULES ON POWER MARKETS 6 (Credit Suisse, 2010), *available at* http://op.bna.com/env.nsf/id/jstn-8actja/$File/suisse.pdf.
[94] Letter from Congressman Fred Upton to Lisa Jackson, Administrator, Environmental Protection Agency (Dec. 3, 2010) (on file with author), *available at* http://upton.house.gov/UploadedFiles/Upton_letter_to_ Admin_Jackson_re_Cooling_Water_Intake_Structu res.pdf.
[95] U.S. ENERGY INFORMATION ADMINISTRATION, ELECTRIC POWER ANNUAL 2009 2 (2011), *available at* http://www.eia.gov/cneaf/electricity/epa/epa.pdf.
[96] Shelley DuBois, *Does the EPA have the tools to regulate fracking?*, CNNMONEY.COM, Oct. 1, 2010, *available at* http://money.cnn.com/2010/10/01/news/companies/EPA_ Clean_Water_Act_fracking.fortune/index.htm.
[97] Mike Soraghan, *Natural Gas: EPA Posts Frack Rules Without Explanation, and Industry Cries Foul*, E&E NEWS GREENWIRE, Jan. 19, 2011, *available at* http://www.eenews.net/ Greenwire/2011/01/19/1/.

[98] Katie Benner & Shelley DuBois, *Odorless, Colorless: The Quiet Rise of American Big Gas*, CNNMONEY.COM, Oct. 1, 2010, *available at* http://money.cnn.com/2010/09/29/news/companies/fracking_ natural_gas_industry.fortune/index.htm.

[99] Katherine Ling, *New EPA Power-Plant Proposals Threaten Reliability – NERC*, E&E NEWS PM, Oct. 26, 2010, *available at* http://www.eenews.net/eenewspm/2010/10/26/1/.

[100] NORTH AMERICAN ELECTRIC RELIABILITY CORPORATION, 2010 SPECIAL RELIABILITY ASSESSMENT: RESOURCE ADEQUACY IMPACTS OF POTENTIAL U.S. ENVIRONMENTAL REGULATIONS 42 (2010), *available at* http://www.nerc.com/files/EPA_Scenario_Final.pdf.

[101] Letter from Thomas R. Kuhn, Edison Electric Institute, to Darrell Issa, Ranking Member, Comm. on Oversight & Gov't Reform 1 (Dec. 30, 2010) (on file with author).

[102] *Id.* at 6.

[103] President Barack Obama, Address on the Economy in Schenectady, New York (Jan. 21, 2011), *available at* http://www.whitehouse.gov/the-press-office/2011/01/21/remarks-presidenteconomy-schenectady-new-york.

[104] President Barack Obama, State of the Union Address (January 25, 2011) *available at* http://www.whitehouse.gov/the-press-office/2011/01/25/remarks-president-state-union-address.

[105] Letter from Jay Timmons, Executive Vice President, National Association of Manufacturers, to Darrell Issa, Chairman, Comm. on Oversight & Gov't Reform 1 (Jan. 7, 2011) (on file with author).

[106] Figures based on calculations from National Accounts Main Aggregates Database, United Nations Statistics Division, *available at* http://unstats.un.org/unsd/snaama/selbasicFast.asp.

[107] Letter from Paul Cicio, President, Industrial Energy Consumers of America, to Darrell Issa, Chairman, Comm. on Oversight & Gov't Reform 4 (Jan. 10, 2011) (on file with author).

[108] Letter from J. Gregg Borchelt, President & CEO, Brick Industry Association, to Darrell Issa, Chairman, Comm. on Oversight & Gov't Reform 1 (Jan. 10, 2011) (on file with author).

[109] *Id.*

[110] *Id.*

[111] *Id.*

[112] *Id.*

[113] *Id.* at 2.

[114] *Id.*

[115] *Id.*

[116] Fact Sheet, National Science Foundation, Nanotechnology (Apr. 1, 2003), *available at* http://www.nsf.gov/news/news_summ.jsp?cntn_id=100602.

[117] Letter from Vincent Caprio, Executive Director, NanoBusiness Alliance, to Darrell Issa, Chairman, Comm. on Oversight & Gov't Reform 2 (Jan. 7, 2011) (on file with author).

[118] Letter from Rosalind Volpe, Executive Director, Silver Nanotechnology Working Group, to Darrell Issa, Chairman, Comm. on Oversight & Gov't Reform 2 (Jan. 14, 2011) (on file with author).

[119] Letter from Robin K. Wiener, President, Institute of Scrap Recycling Industries, to Darrell Issa, Chairman, Comm. on Oversight & Gov't Reform 2 (Jan. 10, 2011) (on file with author).

[120] *Id.* at 1.

[121] *Id.* at 2.

[122] Letter from Dennis J. Hardman, President, APA, to Darrell Issa, Chairman, Comm. on Oversight & Gov't Reform 1 (Jan. 10, 2011) (on file with author).

[123] Letter from Barbara Higgens, Executive Director, Plumbing Manufacturers International, to Darrell Issa, Chairman, Comm. on Oversight & Gov't Reform 1 (Jan. 10, 2011) (on file with author).

[124] *Id.* at 2.

[125] Letter from Roy Hardy, Executive Vice President, Forging Indus. Ass'n, to Darrell Issa, Chairman, Comm. on Oversight & Gov't Reform 2 (Jan. 14, 2011) (on file with author).

[126] Annual Housing Starts (1978-2010), http://www.nahb.org/ generic.aspx?sectionID=819&genericContentID =554&channelID=311 (last visited Jan. 25, 2011).

[127] *Id.*

[128] For additional discussion of EPA's proposed Ozone and PM NAAQS, see section VII.C.3.

[129] *Id.*

[130] *Id.*

[131] *Id.*

[132] Letter from Richard G. Walker, President, American Architectural Manuf. Ass'n, to Darrell Issa, Chairman, Comm. on Oversight & Gov't Reform (Jan. 10, 2011) (on file with the author).

[133] *Id.*

[134] *Id.*

[135] Letter from Scott Lynch, Executive Vice President, Nat'l Lumber and Building Material Dealers Ass'n, to Darrell Issa, Chairman, Comm. on Oversight & Gov't Reform (Jan. 10, 2011) (on file with the author).

[136] Letter from Joseph Stanton, Senior Vice President and Chief Lobbyist, Nat'l Ass'n of Home Builders, to Darrell Issa, Chairman, Comm. on Oversight & Gov't Reform, (Jan. 20, 2011) (on file with the author).

[137] Letter from Stephen E. Sandherr, President, Associated General Contractors of America, to Darrell Issa, Ranking Member, Comm. on Oversight & Gov't Reform (Dec, 30, 2010) (on file with the author).

[138] *Id.*

[139] Letter from Aris Papadopoulos, Chairman of the Board of Directors, Portland Cement Assoc. to Darrell Issa, Chairman, Comm. on Oversight and Gov't. Ref. (Jan. 10, 2010). For further discussion of EPA's regulation of CCR's see section VII.C.6.

[140] For addition discussion of OSHA's I2P2 program, please see section VII.A.2.

[141] Letter from Thomas J. Gibson, American Iron and Steel Inst., to Darrell Issa, Chairman, Comm. on Oversight & Gov't Reform, (Jan. 10, 2011) (on file with the author). For additional discussion of the I2P2 program, see section VII.B.2 of this report.

[142] Letter from Thomas J. Gibson, American Iron and Steel Inst., to Darrell Issa, Chairman, Comm. on Oversight & Gov't Reform (Jan. 10, 2011) (on file with the author).

[143] Letter from Sean Thurman, Senior Manager Regulatory Affairs, Associated Builders and Contractors, Inc., to Darrell Issa, Chairman, Comm. on Oversight & Gov't Reform (Jan. 7, 2011) (on file with the author).

[144] *Id.*

[145] Letter from Karen Kerrigan, CEO, Small Bus. & Entrepreneurship Council, to Darrell Issa, Chairman, Comm. on Oversight & Gov't Reform (Jan. 12, 2011) (on file with the author). For additional discussion on these rules, see section VII.C.1-3.

[146] *Id.*

[147] GREATER NEW ORLEANS INC., A STUDY OF THE ECONOMIC IMPACT OF THE DEEPWATER HORIZON OIL SPILL 5 (2011).

[148] Letter from Susan Eckerly, Senior Vice President, Nat'l Fed'n of Indep. Businesses, to Document Control Office, OPPT, U.S. EPA (July 2, 2010) (on file with author).

[149] Lead; Clearance and Clearance Testing Requirements for the Renovation, Repair, and Painting Program. Potential Effects, http://yosemite.epa.gov/opei/rulegate.nsf/byRIN/2070-AJ57#2 (last visited Jan. 27, 2011).

[150] Letter from Susan Eckerly, Senior Vice President, Nat'l Fed'n of Indep. Businesses, to Document Control Office, OPPT, U.S. EPA (July 2, 2010) (on file with author).

[151] *Id.*

[152] *Id.*

[153] *Id.*

[154] *Id.*

[155] Letter from Karen Kerrigan, CEO, Small Bus. & Entrepreneurship Council, to Darrell Issa, Chairman, Comm. on Oversight & Gov't Reform (Jan. 12, 2011) (on file with the author).

[156] Letter from Ryan Trainer, President, Int'l Sleep Products Ass'n, to Darrell Issa, Chairman, Comm. on Oversight & Gov't Reform (Jan., 11, 2011) (on file with author); letter from David Hastings, Chairman, Nat'l Council of Textile Organizations, to Darrell Issa, Chairman, Comm. on Oversight & Gov't Reform (Jan. 20, 2011) (on file with author).

[157] Letter from Ryan Trainer, President, Int'l Sleep Products Ass'n, to Darrell Issa, Chairman, Comm. on Oversight & Gov't Reform (Jan., 11, 2011) (on file with author).

[158] Letter from David Hastings, Chairman, Nat'l Council of Textile Organizations, to Darrell Issa, Chairman, Comm. on Oversight & Gov't Reform (Jan. 20, 2011) (on file with author).

[159] Tax Increase Prevention and Reconciliation Act of 2005, Pub. L. No. 109-222.

[160] Letter from Matthew L. Evans, Manager Public Advocacy, CompTIA, to Darrell Issa, Chairman, Comm. on Oversight & Gov't Reform (Jan. 7, 2011) (on file with author).

[161] Letter from Karen Kerrigan, CEO, Small Bus. & Entrepreneurship Council, to Darrell Issa, Chairman, Comm. on Oversight & Gov't Reform (Jan. 12, 2011) (on file with author).

[162] Letter from Stephen E. Sandherr, President, Associated Gen. Contractors of America, to Darrell Issa, Ranking Member, Comm. on Oversight & Gov't Reform (Dec. 30, 2010) (on file with author).

[163] Interpretation of OSHA's Provisions for Feasible Administrative or Engineering Controls of Occupational Noise, 75 Fed. Reg. 64,216 (proposed Oct. 19, 2010) (to be codified at 29 C.F.R. pt. 1910, 1926).

[164] *See, i.e.,* Letter from J. Andrew Doyle, President and CEO, American Coatings Association, to Darrell Issa, Chairman, Comm. on Oversight & Gov't Reform 3 (Jan. 10, 2011) (on file with author).

[165] Letter from Bruce A. Steiner, President, American Coke and Coal Chemicals Institute, to Darrell Issa, Chairman, Comm. on Oversight & Gov't Reform 4 (Jan. 10, 2011) (on file with author).

[166] Letter from Jay Timmons National Association of Manufacturers, to Darrell Issa, Chairman, Comm. on Oversight & Gov't Reform 3 (Jan. 7, 2011) (on file with author).

[167] Letter from David Hastings, Chairman, National Council of Textile Organizations, to Darrell Issa, Chairman, Comm. on Oversight & Gov't Reform 4 (Jan. 20, 2011) (on file with author).

[168] Letter from David Tilstone, President, NTMA, Mike Duffin, Executive Director, Precision Machined Products Association, and William E. Gaskin, President, Precision Metalforming Association, to Darrell Issa, Chairman, Comm. on Oversight & Gov't Reform 2 (Jan. 10, 2011) (on file with author).

[169] *See, i.e.,* Letter from Sean Thurman, Senior Manager, Associated Builders and Contractors, to Darrell Issa, Chairman, Comm. on Oversight & Gov't Reform 6–7 (Jan. 7, 2011) (on file with author).

[170] News Release, U.S. Department of Labor, US Department of Labor's OSHA Withdraws Proposed Interpretation on Occupational Noise (Jan. 19, 2011) *available at* http://www.osha.gov/pls/oshaweb/owadisp.show_document?p_table=NEWS_RELEASES &p_id=19119.

[171] Injury and Prevention Program, 75 Fed. Reg. 23,637 (proposed May 4, 2010) (to be codified at C.F.R. pt 1910).

[172] Letter from Jay Timmons National Association of Manufacturers, to Darrell Issa, Chairman, Comm. on Oversight & Gov't Reform 3–4 (Jan. 7, 2011) (on file with author).

[173] *Id.*

[174] Letter from J. Andrew Doyle, President and CEO, American Coatings Association, to Darrell Issa, Chairman, Comm. on Oversight & Gov't Reform 3 (Jan. 10, 2011) (on file with author).

[175] Letter from Thomas J. Gibson, President and CEO, American Iron and Steel Institute, to Darrell Issa, Chairman, Comm. on Oversight & Gov't Reform 6–7 (Jan. 10, 2011) (on file with author).

[176] Letter from Sean Thurman, Senior Manager, Associated Builders and Contractors, to Darrell Issa, Chairman, Comm. on Oversight & Gov't Reform 4 (Jan. 7, 2011) (on file with author).

[177] Letter from Ann Wilson, Senior Vice President, Government Affairs, Motor and Equipment Manufacturers Association, to Darrell Issa, Chairman, Comm. on Oversight & Gov't Reform 3 (Jan. 10, 2011) (on file with author).

[178] Letter from the National Federation of Independent Business, to Darrell Issa, Ranking Member, Comm. on Oversight & Gov't Reform 2 (Dec. 22, 2010) (on file with author).

[179] Occupation Injury and Illness Recording and Reporting Requirements, 75 Fed. Reg. 4728 (proposed Jan. 29, 2010) (to be codified at 29 C.F.R. pt. 1904).

[180] Letter from Sean Thurman, Senior Manager, Associated Builders and Contractors, to Darrell Issa, Chairman, Comm. on Oversight & Gov't Reform 7 (Jan. 7, 2011) (on file with author).

[181] *Id.*

[182] Letter from Bruce A. Steiner, President, American Coke and Coal Chemicals Institute, to Darrell Issa, Chairman, Comm. on Oversight & Gov't Reform 4 (Jan. 10, 2011) (on file with author).

[183] Comments by National Federation of Independent Business to Occupation Injury and Illness Recording and Reporting Requirements, 75 Fed. Reg. 4,728 (proposed Jan. 29, 2010) (to be codified at 29 C.F.R. pt. 1904).

[184] *Id.*

[185] Letter from Aaron Lowe, Vice President, Government Affairs, Automotive Aftermarket Industry Association, to Darrell Issa, Chairman, Comm. on Oversight & Gov't Reform 2 (Jan. 11, 2011) (on file with author); Letter from William E. Allmond, IV, Vice President, Government Relations, Society of Chemical Manufacturers and Affiliates, to Darrell Issa, Chairman, Comm. on Oversight & Gov't Reform 2–3 (Jan. 10, 2011) (on file with author).

[186] News Release, U.S. Department of Labor, U.S. Labor Department's OSHA Temporarily Withdraws Proposed Column for Work-Related Musculoskeletal Disorders, Reaches Out to Small Businesses (Jan. 25, 2011), *available at* http://www.osha.gov/pls/oshaweb/ owadisp.show_document?p_table=NEWS_ RELEASES&p_id =19158.

[187] Consultation Agreements: Proposed Changed to Consultation Procedures, 75 Fed. Reg. 54,064 (proposed Sept. 3, 2010) (to be codified at 29 C.F.R. pt. 1908).

[188] U.S. Dept. of Labor, On-site Consultation, http://www.osha.gov/dcsp/smallbusiness/consult.html (last visited February 4, 2011).

[189] U.S. Dept. of Labor, On-site Consultation, Safety and Health Achievement Recognition Program, http://www.osha.gov/dcsp/smallbusiness/sharp.html (last visited February 4, 2011).

[190] Letter from Joseph K. Doss, President and CEO, International Bottled Water Association, to Darrell Issa, Chairman, Comm. on Oversight & Gov't Reform 4–5 (Jan. 13, 2011) (on file with author).

[191] *Id.*

[192] *See, i.e.,* Letter from J. Andrew Doyle, President and CEO, American Coatings Association, to Darrell Issa, Chairman, Comm. on Oversight & Gov't Reform 3 (Jan. 10, 2011) (on file with author).

[193] Comments by National Federation of Independent Business to Consultation Agreements: Proposed Changed to Consultation Procedures, 75 Fed. Reg. 54,064 (proposed Sept. 3, 2010) (to be codified at 29 C.F.R. pt. 1908).

[194] Id.

[195] Combustible Dust, 74 Fed. Reg. 54334 (proposed Oct. 21, 2009) (to be codified at 29 C.F.R. pt. 1910).

[196] *Id.*

[197] Letter from Walter Robertson, President, American Wire Producers Association, to Darrell Issa, Chairman, Comm. on Oversight & Gov't Reform 2 (Jan. 14, 2011) (on file with author).

[198] Letter from Thomas J. Gibson, President and CEO, American Iron and Steel Institute, to Darrell Issa, Chairman, Comm. on Oversight & Gov't Reform 6 (Jan. 10, 2011) (on file with author); letter from James L. Mallory, Executive Director, President, Non-Ferrous Founders' Society, to Darrell Issa, Chairman, Comm. on Oversight & Gov't Reform 3 (Jan. 13, 2011) (on file with author).

[199] Letter from Scott Lynch, Executive Vice President, National Lumber and Building Material Dealers Association, to Darrell Issa, Chairman, Comm. on Oversight & Gov't Reform 3 (Jan. 10, 2011) (on file with author).

[200] Letter from Donna Harman, President and CEO, American Forest & Paper Association, to Darrell Issa, Chairman, Comm. on Oversight & Gov't Reform 4 (Jan. 10, 2011) (on file with author).

[201] Exec. Order No. 13,502, 24 C.F.R. 5 (2009).

[202] Use of Project Labor Agreements for Federal Construction Projects, 48 C.F.R. § 536.271 (2010).

[203] Letter from Sean Thurman, Senior Manager, Associated Builders and Contractors, to Darrell Issa, Chairman, Comm. on Oversight & Gov't Reform 2 (Jan. 7, 2011) (on file with author).

[204] *Id.*

[205] *Id.*

[206] *Id.* Letter from Mark A. Casso, President, Construction Industry Round Table, to Darrell Issa, Chairman, Comm. on Oversight & Gov't Reform 4 (Jan. 6, 2011) (on file with author).

[207] Dodd-Frank Wall Street Reform and Consumer Protection Act, Pub. L. No., 111-203, H.R. 4173, 111th Cong. (2010).

[208] U.S. Chamber of Commerce, Center for Capital Markets, Dodd-Frank Wall Street Reform and Consumer Protection Act of 2010: Regulatory Authority, http://www.centerforcapital markets.com/resources/dodd-frank-wall-street-reform-and-consumerprotection-act-of-2010-regulatory-authority/ (last visited Feb. 4, 2011).

[209] DAVID S. EVANS & JOSHUA D. WRIGHT, THE EFFECT OF THE CONSUMER FINANCIAL PROTECTION AGENCY ACT OF 2009 ON CONSUMER CREDIT (Jan. 7, 2010).

[210] *Id.*

[211] Dodd-Frank Wall Street Reform and Consumer Protection Act, Pub. L. No., 111-203, H.R. 4173, 111th Cong. §1075 (2010).

[212] Tim Chen, *Fed Looks to Cap Debit Interchange, Checking Institutions Cringe*, FORBES, Jan. 7, 2011, *available at* http://blogs.forbes.com/moneybuilder/2011/01/07/fed-looks-to-cap-debit-interchangechecking-institutions-cringe/?boxes=Homepagechannels.

[213] Letter from Steve Bartlett, President and CEO, Financial Services Roundtable, to Darrell Issa, Chairman, Comm. on Oversight & Gov't Reform 1 (Jan. 9, 2011) (on file with author).

[214] Letter from Karen Kerrigan, President and CEO, Small Business & Entrepreneurship Council, to Darrell Issa, Chairman, Comm. on Oversight & Gov't Reform 7 (Jan. 12, 2011) (on file with author).

[215] Letter from Bill Cheney, President and CEO, Credit Union National Association, to Darrell Issa, Chairman, Comm. on Oversight & Gov't Reform 1 (Jan. 5, 2011) (on file with author).

[216] *Id.*

[217] Dodd-Frank Wall Street Reform and Consumer Protection Act, Pub. L. No., 111-203, H.R. 4173, 111th Cong. §1001-1100 (2010).

[218] DAVID S. EVANS & JOSHUA D. WRIGHT, THE EFFECT OF THE CONSUMER FINANCIAL PROTECTION AGENCY ACT OF 2009 ON CONSUMER CREDIT, (Jan. 7, 2010).

[219] Letter from Bill Himpler, Executive Vice President, American Financial Services Association, to Darrell Issa, Chairman, Comm. on Oversight & Gov't Reform 1 (Jan. 27, 2011) (on file with author).

[220] *Id.*

[221] Letter from Stuart Blatt, President, Debt Buying Association International, to Darrell Issa, Chairman, Comm. on Oversight & Gov't Reform 1 (Jan. 10, 2011) (on file with author).

[222] Fair Debt Collection Practices Act, Pub. L. 109-351, §§ 801–2, 120 Stat. 1966 (2006).

[223] Letter from Larry Burton, Executive Director, Business Roundtable, to Darrell Issa, Chairman, Comm. on Oversight & Gov't Reform 3-Attachment (Jan. 7, 2011) (on file with author).

[224] Facilitating Shareholder Director Nominations, 17 C.F.R. §240.12b-2 (2010).

[225] Letter from Larry Burton, Executive Director, Business Roundtable, to Darrell Issa, Chairman, Comm. on Oversight & Gov't Reform 3-Attachment (Jan. 7, 2011) (on file with author).

[226] Business Roundtable v. SEC, No. 10-1035 (D.C. Cir. filed on Nov. 30, 2010).

[227] SEC Order Granting Stay of Commission's Facilitating Shareholder Director's Nomination Rules, File No. S7-10-09, *available at* http://www.sec.gov/rules/other/2010/33-9149.pdf.

[228] Conflict Minerals, 74 Fed. Reg. 80948 (proposed Dec. 23, 2010) (to be codified at 17 C.F.R. pt. 229, 249).

[229] *Id.*

[230] *Id.*

[231] *Id.*

[232] Jessica Holzer, SEC Proposes 'Conflict Mineral' Report, WALL ST J. (Dec. 16, 2010), available at http://online.wsj.com/article/SB10001424052748704098304576021884130820122.html.

[233] Letter from Jay Timmons, Executive Vice President, National Association of Manufacturers, to Darrell Issa, Chairman, Comm. on Oversight & Gov't Reform (Jan. 7, 2011) (on file with author).

[234] Letter from Larry Burton, Executive Director, Business Roundtable, to Darrell Issa, Chairman, Comm. on Oversight & Gov't Reform 2 (Jan. 7, 2011) (on file with author).

[235] Letter from Dennis P. McGuirk, President, IPC-Association Connecting Electronic Industries, to Darrell Issa, Chairman, Comm. on Oversight & Gov't Reform 3 (Jan. 7, 2011) (on file with author).

[236] Letter from Red Cavaney, Senior Vice President, Government Affairs, Conoco Phillips, to Darrell Issa, Chairman, Comm. on Oversight & Gov't Reform (Jan. 5, 2011) (on file with author).

[237] Letter from Christine M. Cochrane, President, Commodity Markets Council, to Darrell Issa, Chairman, Comm. on Oversight & Gov't Reform 1 (Jan. 14, 2011) (on file with author).

[238] *Id.*

[239] Dodd-Frank Wall Street Reform and Consumer Protection Act § 723(7)(A), Pub. L. No., 111-203, H.R. 4173, 111th Cong. (2010).

[240] End-User Exception to Mandatory Clearing of Swaps, 75 Fed. Reg. 80747 (proposed Dec. 23, 2010) (to be codified at 17 C.F.R. pt. 39). John Carney, *Will the CFTC Kill the End User Exemption?* CNBC, October 4, 2010, *available at* http://www.cnbc.com/id/39506763/Will_The_CFTC_Kill_The_End_User_Exemption.

[242] *Id.*

[243] Ian Katz and Robert Schmidt, *Gensler Turns Back on Wall Street to Push Derivatives Overhaul*, BLOOMBERG, February 12, 2010, *available at* http://www.bloomberg.com/apps/news?pid=newsarchive& sid=a3OkrdITAZtA.

[244] John Carney, Will the CTC Kill the End User Exemption?, CNBC, October 4, 2010, available at http://www.cnbc.com/id/39506763/Will_The_CFTC_Kill_The_End_User_Exemption.

[245] Letter from Coalition for Derivatives End-Users to Harry Reid, Majority Leader, Senate (Feb. 3, 2010) (*available at* http://www.sec.gov/comments/s7-16-10/s71610-6.pdf).

[246] Letter from Larry Burton, Executive Director, Business Roundtable, to Darrell Issa, Chairman, Comm. on Oversight & Gov't Reform, Attachment, 4–5 (Jan. 7, 2011) (on file with author).

[247] KEYBRIDGE RESEARCH, AN ANALYSIS OF THE BUSINESS ROUNDTABLE'S SURVEY ON OVER-THE-COUNTER DERIVATIVES (April 14, 2010).

[248] Letter from Jay Timmons, Executive Vice President, National Association of Manufacturers, to Darrell Issa, Chairman, Comm. on Oversight & Gov't Reform 2 (Jan. 7, 2011) (on file with author).

[249] *Id.*

[250] *Id.*

[251] Letter from Red Cavaney, Senior Vice President, Government Affairs, Conoco Phillips, to Darrell Issa, Chairman, Comm. on Oversight & Gov't Reform (Jan. 5, 2011) (on file with author).

[252] Letter from Barry Russell, President and CEO, Independent Petroleum Association of America, to Darrell Issa, Ranking Member, Comm. on Oversight & Gov't Reform 2 (Dec. 27, 2010) (on file with author).

[253] *Id.*

[254] JAMES E. MCCARTHY, CONGRESSIONAL RESEARCH SERVICE, EPA'S BOILER MACT: CONTROLLING EMISSIONS OF HAZARDOUS AIR POLLUTANTS (Jan. 24, 2011), *available at* http://www.crs.gov/Products/R/PDF/R41459.pdf.

[255] *Id.*

[256] *Id.*

[257] COUNCIL OF INDUS. BOILER OWNERS, THE ECONOMIC IMPACT OF PROPOSED EPA BOILER/PROCESS HEATER MACT RULE ON INDUSTRIAL, COMMERCIAL, AND INSTITUTIONAL BOILER AND PROCESS HEATER OPERATIONS 7 (2010).

[258] Study Says EPA Boiler MACT Rule Would Destroy tens of thousands of US Pulp and Paper Jobs, http://www.risiinfo.com/techchannels/powerenergy/Study-says-EPA-Boiler-MACT-rule-wouldu2018destroyu2019-tens-of-thousands-of-US-pulp-and-paper-jobs.html (last visited Feb. 4. 2011).

[259] *Id.*

[260] Letter from William L. Kovacs, U.S. Chamber of Commerce, to Darrell Issa, Ranking Member, Comm. on Oversight & Gov't Reform, (Dec. 29, 2011) (on file with author).

[261] Letter from Bill Perdue, VP Regulatory Affairs, American Home Furnishings Alliance, to Darrell Issa, Chairman, Comm. on Oversight & Gov't Reform, (Jan. 10, 2011) (on file with author).

[262] Comments from NFIB to U.S. EPA, Docket IDs: EPA-HQ-OAR-2006-0790; EPA-HQ-OAR-2003- 0119 (Aug. 18, 2010).

[263] Gabriel Nelson, *Draft Rules for Boilers Were Too Strict, EPA Air Chief Says*, N.Y. TIMES, Dec. 2, 2010, http://www.nytimes.com/gwire/2010/12/02/02greenwire-draft-air-pollution-rules-for-boilers-weretoo-79802.html.

[264] *Id.*

[265] Massachusetts v. EPA, 549 U.S. 497 (2007).

[266] Memorandum from Stephen L. Johnson, Administrator, U.S. EPA, to Regional Administrators, (Dec. 18, 2008) (available at http://www.epa.gov/NSR/documents/psd_interpretive_memo_12.18.08.pdf).

[267] U.S. EPA, Reconsideration of Interpretation of Regulations that Determine Pollutants Covered by Clean Air Act Permitting Programs (Mar. 2010) (http://www.epa.gov/NSR/documents/psd_memo_recon_032910.pdf).

[268] Clean Air Act § 101, 41 U.S.C § 7401 et seq.

[269] 75 Fed. Reg. 25,324 (May 7, 2011).

[270] Letter from Susan M. Walthall, et al., Acting Chief Counsel, Office of Advocacy, Small Business Admin, to Lisa P. Jackson, Administrator, U.S. EPA, (Dec. 23, 2009) (http://archive.sba.gov/advo/laws/ comments/epa09_1223.html).

[271] 75 Fed. Reg. 77,698 (Dec. 13, 2010).

[272] Letter from Carmen Haworth, Public Policy Counsel, Agricultural Resources Assoc., to Darrell Issa, Chairman, Comm. on Oversight & Gov't Reform (Jan. 11, 2011) (on file with author).

[273] Letter from J. Gregg Borchelt, President and CEO, Brick Indus. Assoc., to Darrell Issa, Chairman, Comm. on Oversight & Gov't Reform (Jan. 10, 2011) (on file with author).

[274] *Id.*

[275] Letter from Roy Hardy, Executive Vice President, Forging Indus. Ass'n, to Darrell Issa, Chairman, Comm. on Oversight & Gov't Reform 2 (Jan. 14, 2011) (on file with author).

[276] Letter from William L. Kovacs, U.S. Chamber of Commerce, to Darrell Issa, Ranking Member, Comm. on Oversight & Gov't Reform (Dec. 29, 2011) (on file with author).

[277] LARRY PARKER & JAMES E. MCCARTHY, CONGRESSIONAL RESEARCH SERVICE, EPA'S BACT GUIDANCE FOR GHGS FROM STATIONARY SOURCES (Nov. 22, 2010), *available at* http://www.fas.org/sgp/crs/misc/R41505.pdf.

[278] Letter from Thomas J. Gibson, American Iron and Steel Inst., to Darrell Issa, Chairman, Comm. on Oversight & Gov't Reform (Jan. 10, 2011) (on file with author).

[279] *Id.*

[280] *Id.*

[281] *Id.*

[282] Letter from Phillip D. Brady, President Nat'l Automobile Dealers Assoc., to Darrell Issa, Chairman, Comm. on Oversight & Gov't Reform (Jan. 5, 2011) (on file with author).

[283] *Id.*

[284] Letter from Joseph F. Rajkovacz, Dir. of Regulatory Affairs, Owner-Operator Indep. Drivers Assoc.
to Darrell Issa, Chairman, Comm. on Oversight & Gov't Reform (Jan. 10, 2011) (on file with the author).

[285] *Id.*

[286] *Id.*

[287] Letter from Ann Wilson, Senior Vice President Gov't Affairs, Motor & Equip. Manufacturers Assoc., to Darrell Issa, Chairman, Comm. on Oversight & Gov't Affairs (Jan. 10, 2011) (on file with author).

[288] Letter from Shane Karr, Vice President Fed. Gov't Affairs, Alliance of Auto. Manufacturers, to Darrell Issa, Chairman, Comm. on Oversight & Gov't Reform (Jan. 11, 2011) (on file with author).

[289] *Id.*

[290] Letter from Peter Lawson, Vice President, Government Relations, Ford Motor Co. to Darrell Issa, Chairman, Comm. on Oversight & Gov't Reform 7 (Jan. 12, 201) (on file with author).

[291] Letter from William L. Kovacs, Senior Vice President, Environment, Technology & Regulatory Affairs, U.S. Chamber of Commerce, to Darrell Issa, Ranking Member, Comm. on Oversight & Gov't Reform 7 (Dec. 29, 2010) (on file with author).

[292] Letter from Dr. Jonathan M. Samet, Chair, Clean Air Scientific Advisory Committee to Lisa Jackson, Administrator, Environmental Protection Agency i-ii (September 10, 2010) (*available at* http://www.epa.gov/casac).

[293] Letter from Donna Harman, President & CEO, American Forest & Paper Association, to Darrell Issa, Chairman, Comm. on Oversight & Gov't Reform 2 (Jan. 10, 2011) (on file with author).

[294] *Id.*

[295] *Id.*

[296] Letter from Bruce A. Steiner, President, American Coke and Chemicals Institute, to Darrell Issa, Chairman, Comm. on Oversight & Gov't Reform 2 (Jan. 10, 2011) (on file with author).

[297] *Id.* at 1.

[298] Letter from Jennifer Joy Wilson, President and CEO, National Sand, Stone & Gravel, to Darrell Issa, Chairman, Comm. on Oversight & Gov't Reform, Attachment, 5 (Jan. 7, 2011) (on file with author).

[299] Letter from Bob Stallman, President, American Farm Bureau Federation, to Darrell Issa, Chairman, Comm. on Oversight & Gov't Reform, Attachment 10 (Jan. 10, 2011) (on file with author).

[300] Letter from Jennifer Joy Wilson, President and CEO, National Sand, Stone & Gravel, to Darrell Issa, Chairman, Comm. on Oversight & Gov't Reform, Attachment, 5 (Jan. 7, 2011) (on file with author).

[301] *Id.* at 6.

[302] *Id.*

[303] Clean Air Act § 109, 42 U.S.C. § 7409.

[304] Letter from William L. Kovacs, Senior Vice President, Environment, Technology & Regulatory Affairs, U.S. Chamber of Commerce, to Darrell Issa, Ranking Member, Comm. on Oversight & Gov't Reform 4-5 (Dec. 29, 2010) (on file with author).

[305] Fact Sheet from the Environmental Protection Agency, Proposal to Revise the National Ambient Air Quality Standards for Ozone 2 (Jan. 6, 2010) *available at* http://www.epa.gov/glo/pdfs/fs20100106std.pdf.

[306] MINORITY STAFF, UNITED STATES SENATE COMMITTEE ON ENVIRONMENT AND PUBLIC WORKS, EPA'S ANTI-INDUSTRIAL POLICY: THREATENING JOBS AND AMERICA'S MANUFACTURING BASE 8 (2010).

[307] Letter from Jennifer Joy Wilson, President and CEO, National Sand, Stone & Gravel, to Darrell Issa, Chairman, Comm. on Oversight & Gov't Reform, Attachment, 5 (Jan. 7, 2011) (on file with author).

[308] *Id.*

[309] U.S. ENVIRONMENTAL PROTECTION AGENCY, CHESAPEAKE BAY TMDL EXECUTIVE SUMMARY 1 (2010).

[310] *Id.*

[311] *Id.*

[312] *Id.* at 1-2.

[313] *Id.* at 3.

[314] Chesapeake Bay TMDL Action Timeline, U.S. EPA, http://www.epa.gov/reg3wapd/tmdl/ChesapeakeBay/EnsuringResults.html?tab2=7#2011 (last visited Jan. 31, 2011).

[315] Interview with Aaron Hobbs, President, Responsible Indus. for Sound Env't, in Wash., D.C. (Jan. 31, 2011).

[316] Letter from Bob Stallman, President, American Farm Bureau Federation, to Darrell Issa, Chairman, Comm. on Oversight & Gov't Reform, Attachment, 10 (Jan. 10, 2011) (on file with author).

[317] Letter from Carmen Haworth, Public Policy Counsel, Agricultural Retailers Assoc., to Darrell Issa, Chairman, Comm. on Oversight & Gov't Reform (Jan. 11, 2011) (on file with author).

[318] *Id.*

[319] Letter from Donna Harman, President & CEO, American Forest & Paper Association, to Darrell Issa, Chairman, Comm. on Oversight & Gov't Reform 2 (Jan. 10, 2011) (on file with author).

[320] *Id.*

[321] Letter from Dave Tenny, Nat'l Alliance of Forest Owners, to Darrell Issa, Chairman, Comm. on Oversight & Gov't Reform, (Jan. 10, 2011) (on file with author).

[322] Interview with Aaron Hobbs, President, Responsible Indus. for Sound Env't, in Wash., D.C. (Jan. 31, 2011).

[323] *Id.*

[324] *Id.*

[325] Clean Water Act, 33 U.S.C. §316(b).

[326] NORTH AMERICAN ELECTRIC RELIABILITY CORPORATION, 2010 SPECIAL ASSESSMENT: RESOURCE ADEQUACY IMPACTS OF POTENTIAL U.S. ENVIRONMENTAL REGULATIONS 46 (2010).

[327] *Id.*

[328] Letter from Larry Burton, Executive Director, Business Roundtable, to Darrell Issa, Chairman, Comm. on Oversight & Gov't Reform 2-attachment (Jan. 7, 2011) (on file with author).

[329] *Id.*

[330] Letter from Lisa Jackson, Environmental Protection Agency, to Fred Upton, Congressman (Dec. 16, 2010) (on file with author).

[331] Letter from Thomas R. Kuhn, Edison Electric Institute, to Darrell Issa, Ranking Member, Comm. On Oversight & Gov't Reform 2–3 (Dec. 30, 2010) (on file with author).

[332] Letter from Robert E. Murray, Murray Energy Corporation, Chairman, President and Chief Executive Officer, to Darrell Issa, Ranking Member, Comm. on Oversight & Gov't Reform, Attachment, 5 (Dec. 31, 2010) (on file with author).

[333] Letter from Thomas R. Kuhn, Edison Electric Institute, to Darrell Issa, Ranking Member, Comm. on Oversight & Gov't Reform 3 (Dec. 30, 2010) (on file with author).

[334] Letter from William L. Kovacs, Senior Vice President, Environment, Technology & Regulatory Affairs, U.S. Chamber of Commerce, to Darrell Issa, Ranking Member, Comm. on Oversight & Gov't Reform 5 (Dec. 29, 2010) (on file with author).

[335] Letter from Aris Papadopoulos, Chairman of the Board of Directors, Portland Cement Association, to Darrell Issa, Chairman, Comm. on Oversight & Gov't Reform, Attachment, 6 (Feb. 1, 2011) (on file with author).

[336] *Id.* at 8.

[337] *Id.* at 16.

[338] Letter from Donna Harman, President & CEO, American Forest & Paper Association, to Darrell Issa, Chairman, Comm. on Oversight & Gov't Reform 4 (Jan. 10, 2011) (on file with author).

[339] LINDA LUTHER, CONGRESSIONAL RESEARCH SERVICE, MANAGING COAL COMBUSTION WASTE (CCW): ISSUES WITH DISPOSAL AND USE 3 (2010).

[340] 76 Fed. Reg. 4,662 (Jan. 26, 2011).

[341] *Id.*

[342] Regulatory Announcement E15 Partial Waiver, U.S. EPA Office of Transportation and Air Quality, (2011).

[343] *Id.*

[344] *Id.*

[345] Interview with Shane Karr, Vice President Federal Gov't Affiar, Alliance of Auto. Manufacturers (Jan. 31, 2011).

[346] *Id.*

[347] *Id.*

[348] Letter from Phillip D. Brady, President, Nat'l Auto. Dealers Ass'n, to Darrell Issa, Chairman, Comm. on Oversight & Gov't Reform (Jan. 5, 2011) (on file with author).

[349] *Id.*

[350] *Id.*

[351] Letter from Thomas J. Lehner, Vice President, Gov't & Indus. Affairs, Toyota Motor N. America to Darrell Issa Chairman, Comm. on Oversight & Gov't Reform (Jan. 10, 2011) (on file with author).

[352] *Id.*

[353] *Id.*

[354] Letter from Charles T. Drevna, President, Nat'l Petrochemical and Refiners Ass'n, to Darrell Issa Chairman, Comm. on Oversight & Gov't Reform (Jan. 10, 2011) (on file with author).

[355] Interview with Shane Karr, Vice President Federal Gov't Affairs, Alliance of Auto. Manufacturers (Jan, 31, 2011) (on file with author).

[356] Letter from Charles T. Drevna, President, Nat'l Petrochemical and Refiners Ass'n, to Darrell Issa Chairman, Comm. on Oversight & Gov't Reform (Jan. 10, 2011) (on file with author).

[357] Letter from Cindy L. Squires Chief Counsel for Public Affairs, Nat'l Marine Manufacturers Ass'n, to Darrell Issa, Chairman, Comm. on Oversight & Gov't Reform (Jan. 19, 2011) (on file with author).

[358] *Id.*

[359] *Id.*

[360] 75 Fed. Reg. 24,851 (May 6, 2010).

[361] 40 C.F.R § 745 (2011).

[362] 75 Fed. Reg. 24,802 (May 6, 2010).

[363] *Id.*

[364] 75 Fed. Reg. 24,851 (May 6, 2010).

[365] 75 Fed. Reg. 25,038 (May 6, 2010).

[366] Letter from Richard G. Walker , President and CEO, American Architectural Manufacturers Ass'n to Darrell Issa, Chairman, Comm. on Oversight & Gov't Reform (Jan. 10, 2011) (on file with author); Letter from Air Conditioning Contractors of America, et. al, to Darrell Issa, Chairman Comm. on Oversight & Gov't Reform (Jan. 10, 2011) (on file with the author).

[367] Letter from Richard G. Walker , President and CEO, American Architectural Manufacturers Ass'n to Darrell Issa, Chairman, Comm. on Oversight & Gov't Reform (Jan. 10, 2011) (on file with the author).

[368] Letter from Susan M. Walthall, et al., Office of Advocacy, Small Bus. Admin., to Hon. Lisa Jackson, Administrator, U.S. EPA, (Nov. 27, 2009) (on file with author).

[369] Letter from Air Conditioning Contractors of America, et. al, to Darrell Issa, Chairman Comm. on Oversight & Gov't Reform (Jan. 10, 2011) (on file with the author).

[370] *Id.*

[371] *Id.*

[372] *Id.*

[373] Letter from Stephen E. Sandherr, President, Associated General Contractors of America, to Darrell Issa, Ranking Member, Comm. on Oversight & Gov't Reform (Dec, 30, 2010) (on file with the author).

[374] *Id.*

[375] Letter from Air Conditioning Contractors of America, et. al, to Darrell Issa, Chairman, Comm. on Oversight & Gov't Reform (Jan. 10, 2011) (on file with the author).

[376] Letter from Scott Lynch, Executive Vice President, Nat'l Lumber and Building Material Dealers Ass'n, to Darrell Issa, Chairman, Comm. on Oversight & Gov't Reform, (Jan. 10, 2011) (on file with the author).

[377] *Id.*

[378] *Id.*

[379] FINAL DETERMINATION OF THE U.S. ENVIRONMENTAL PROTECTION AGENCY PURSUANT TO §404(C) OF THE CLEAN WATER ACT CONCERNING THE SPRUCE NO. 1 MINE, LOGAN COUNTY, WEST VIRGINIA, U.S. ENVIRONMENTAL PROTECTION AGENCY 6 (2011).

[380] *Id.* at 19.

[381] *Id.* at 6.

[382] Memorandum, Detailed Guidance: Improving EPA Review of Appalachian Surface Coal Mining Operations under the Clean Water Act, National Environmental Policy Act, and the Environmental Justice Executive Order, U.S. Environmental Protection Agency, Apr. 1, 2010.

[383] Letter from Karen Bennett, Vice President, Env. Affairs, Nat'l Mining Ass'n, to Darrell Issa, Chairman, Comm. on Oversight & Gov't Reform (Jan. 6, 2011) (on file with author).

[384] *Id.*

[385] NMA v. Jackson, No. 10-1220, slip op. at 20-21 (D. D.C. Jan. 14, 2011).

[386] Letter from Karen Bennett, Vice President, Env. Affairs, Nat'l Mining Ass'n, to Darrell Issa, Chairman, Comm. on Oversight & Gov't Reform, (Jan. 6, 2011) (on file with author).

[387] *Id.*

[388] Letter from Waters Advoc.Coalition, to Nancy Helen Sutley, Chair, Council on Env. Quality (Jan. 12, 2011) (on file with author).

[389] *Id.*

Assessing Impediments of Job Creation
Editor: Joshua A. Lancolm
ISBN: 978-1-61324-352-7

Chapter 2

TESTIMONY OF JAY TIMMONS, PRESIDENT & CEO, NATIONAL ASSOCIATION OF MANUFACTURERS, BEFORE THE COMMITTEE ON OVERSIGHT & GOVERNMENT REFORM, U.S. HOUSE OF REPRESENTATIVES ON "REGULATORY IMPEDIMENTS TO JOB CREATION"*

Chairman Issa, Ranking Member Cummings and members of the Committee on Oversight & Government Reform, thank you for the opportunity to testify before you today about the impact of regulation on job creation and the economy.

My name is Jay Timmons, and I am president and CEO of the National Association of Manufacturers (NAM). The NAM is the nation's largest manufacturing trade association, representing manufacturers in every industrial sector and in all 50 states. Manufacturing has a presence in every single congressional district providing good, high-paying jobs. The United States is the world's largest manufacturing economy. It produces $1.6 trillion of value each year, or 11.2 percent of GDP, and employs nearly 12 million Americans working directly in manufacturing.

* These remarks were delivered as testimony given before the Committee on Oversight and Government Reform on February 10, 2011. Jay Timmons is President and CEO of National Association of Manufacturers.

This is my first opportunity to testify before a congressional committee since I assumed my duties as president of the NAM in January. Manufacturing is deeply important to me personally as well as professionally. During the Great Depression, my grandfather stood in line for months to get a job at a local manufacturing plant in Chillicothe, Ohio. It was that job, and manufacturing jobs like it, that helped create and strengthen the middle class in this country and made it possible for my own family to succeed. In my current role, it is my honor and privilege to fight for the opportunity for other families to hold good-paying manufacturing jobs like the one my grandfather was so determined to get decades ago.

On behalf of the NAM and the millions of men and women working in manufacturing in the United States, I wish to express my support for your efforts to bring greater oversight to the cumulative burden of regulation the economy now faces and to examine the specific costly proposals coming from this and previous administrations.

Manufacturing has been deeply affected by the most recent recession. This sector lost 2.2 million jobs since the recession began in December 2007. The United States finished the year with a net gain of 136,000 manufacturing jobs – a definitive positive, yet only 6.2 percent of the sector's total losses in the recession. To regain manufacturing momentum and encourage hiring, the United States needs not just improved economic conditions but also government policies more attuned to the realities of global competition. It is because of the significant challenges affecting manufacturing in the United States that the NAM developed a strategy to enhance our growth.

The NAM published its "Manufacturing Strategy for Jobs and a Competitive America" in June of last year. In that strategy, we identified three overarching objectives: 1) to be the best country in the world to headquarter a company; 2) to be the best country in the world to do the bulk of a company's research and development; and 3) to be a great place to manufacture goods and export products. To achieve those objectives, we need sound policies in taxation, energy, labor, trade, health care, education and, certainly, regulation.

Unfortunately, over the last two years, we have not seen sensible and cost-beneficial regulation being proposed by government agencies. On the contrary, an aggressive federal bureaucracy has imposed unworkable and excessive regulations with little regard for their impact on job creation and the economy. This hearing is critically important to help change the dynamic among the regulators and to bring accountability to the Executive Branch.

The NAM welcomed the very clear, new direction on regulation announced by President Obama in his op-ed in *The Wall Street Journal*, through his Executive Order 13563 and his memorandum on small business regulatory flexibility.

With that new direction, a clean-up of sorts is necessary. Congress and the Administration should scrutinize the past two years of regulations and those currently under consideration to determine if they are consistent with a national mission of jobs and economic growth. We must note that some agencies are guilty of an agenda of overreach and insensitivity to costs and small businesses.

One particularly striking example of the overreach is the recent attempt by the Occupational Safety and Health Administration (OSHA) to reinterpret the definition of "feasible administrative or engineering controls" with regard to noise standards. Manufacturing facilities can be noisy places with the shaping and machining of metal, welding, cutting and other processes. The safety of our workers is a critical responsibility of manufacturers, both as a moral duty but also to preserve the effectiveness of those workers. It is in our best interests to take care of our employees, and that includes protecting their hearing.

Since 1983, OSHA has had an enforcement policy that accepted employers' use of personal protective equipment, such as ear plugs and other ear protection along with a hearing conservation program, when it is less costly than administrative or engineering controls. This reasonable approach means manufacturers did not have to redesign facilities, buy costly new systems or get rid of expensive machines if workers could be protected with personal protective equipment. OSHA set a standard and expected employers to use the most cost-effective approach. This is not radical and, in fact, is exactly the kind of common-sense approach embodied in the President's new Executive Order 13563.

The new Executive Order suggests that benefits must justify costs, that regulations should be tailored to impose the least burden on society, that the regulatory option chosen should create the most net benefits, and that performance objectives should guide the rules rather than a particular method of compliance. In October, OSHA proposed to do the exact opposite of those principles by reinterpreting the word "feasible" with regard to this standard from cost-beneficial to achievable "if they will not threaten the employer's ability to remain in business." So instead of this being a discussion of whether regulations affect job creation, OSHA demands that a company demonstrate it would go out of business if it had to use more costly methods. There is no indication that the more costly methods would better protect workers, just that the agency feels it has the authority to impose them.

This is an example of bureaucratic inflexibility and excess on the part of OSHA, directly contrasting the principles the President has outlined to be sensitive to the impact of regulations on jobs, the economy and especially small businesses. We have been gathering data from our members on the potential costs of this reinterpretation of the word "feasible", and our preliminary findings are that the range of costs imposed on businesses is from hundreds of thousands of dollars for the smallest of companies, millions of dollars for many medium-sized operations, to one company's estimate of a *one billion dollar compliance cost.* Now, these costs might not put every one of those companies out of business, but the new demands would divert scarce capital while providing no new benefit to our workers. How could any government agency think this made sense? How could any government agency not appreciate the fragility of the economic recovery and what this would do to job creation?

Thankfully, OSHA withdrew this proposal on January 19 of this year, just one day after publication of the President's new Executive Order. OSHA has decided to suspend work on this proposal while it investigates other options to achieve its objectives, but it has not pledged to eliminate this option from future consideration. Congressional oversight is still crucial to make sure this bad idea does not re-emerge.

In the same press release announcing the withdrawal, OSHA reminds small businesses of its on-site consultation program that offers free and confidential advice to help make workplaces safer. What the release fails to mention is that OSHA is in the process of proposing amendments to that program that would remove the "wall of separation" between the consultation program and the enforcement staff. OSHA's actions here will only serve to discourage small businesses from participating in this successful program by making it more likely that a confidential consultation will turn into a surprise enforcement referral for something that does not present an imminent danger. OSHA is headed in the wrong direction with yet another proposal and needs Congress and other stakeholders to help right the ship.

The Environment Protection Agency (EPA) is also a significant contributor to costly and unnecessary burdens placed on the economy. The burden of environmental regulation falls disproportionately on manufacturers and is heaviest on small manufacturers because the compliance costs are not affected by economies of scale. Even our smallest members require one or two staff dedicated full-time to regulatory compliance, especially for environmental regulations. Often, manufacturers feel compelled to hire additional expensive consultants to help stay abreast of all the new and changing requirements. But this is just one part of the challenge facing manufacturers.

The EPA has been embarked on a decades-long process to implement the Clean Air Act and its amendments. There is no doubt that enormous benefits have been brought to our nation from efforts to improve air quality. But the continued ratcheting down of emission limits produces diminishing returns at far higher marginal costs. This means that each new air rule will have a greater impact on job creation than those in the past.

Costs of pollution abatement are capital intensive. In a time of economic recovery where capital is extremely scarce, every dollar diverted from productive use creates additional pressure to reduce labor costs. And when commodities and other manufacturing inputs are increasing in costs, even more pressure builds to squeeze labor costs. In this environment, it is very clear that unnecessary or cost-ineffective regulation will dampen economic growth and will continue to hold down job creation. For some firms it will be the final marginal straw that destroys the whole business.

That is why it is so shocking that the EPA decided to take a Bush Administration rule that was enormously costly, the National Ambient Air Quality Standard (NAAQS) for Ozone, and propose making it even more stringent and costly. One study by the Manufacturers Allliance/MAPI estimated the most stringent proposal would result in the loss of 7.3 million jobs by 2020 and add \$1 trillion in new regulatory costs per year between 2020 and 2030. We have a short reprieve from this rule because the EPA has delayed its final proposal until July. But Congress must work with the EPA to stop the agency from making a \$1 trillion mistake.

If the traditional challenges with air quality regulations were not enough to discourage manufacturers from hiring new employees or investing in new equipment, then the decision to regulate carbon dioxide (CO2) as a pollutant under the Clean Air Act certainly will. This is unlike any regulation manufacturers have ever experienced. In the past, technology has helped to develop cheaper methods to "scrub" pollutants from our smokestacks. But CO2 cannot be scrubbed from emissions; it can only be reduced through reductions in output or fuel switching. The easiest way to reduce CO2 from stationary sources is to reduce economic output. That is a recipe for job losses. And although these regulations start with the largest facilities, the stage has been set to regulate even the smallest manufacturers. The possibility creates an overhang of uncertainty that casts a dark shadow on the future of manufacturing in this country. Congress must act quickly to eliminate this threat and reclaim its authority to determine how CO2 will be regulated and stop the EPA from abusing the intent of the Clean Air Act for this purpose.

The cumulative burden of these new and costly regulations is nearing a tipping point. The 112th Congress has the ability to recognize the dangerous course we are on and to change it before it is too late for our economy and the American worker. This Committee enjoys a unique jurisdictional mandate to look over the entirety of the federal government and its regulatory programs. Only through a wide focus can the true scope of the impacts on manufacturing and job creation be seen clearly. We welcome your commitment to this effort. And we welcome the President's expressed commitment to be sensitive toward the impact of future regulations. But looking forward is not enough. For the sake of economic vitality, an emphasis on reasonable regulation must also examine recently contemplated, proposed and finalized rules.

Allow me to reiterate manufacturers' concerns with several additional regulatory programs that have not been sufficiently rethought or that are still headed in a troubling direction.

EPA Boiler MACT

The EPA has proposed a rule that would establish more stringent emissions standards on industrial and commercial boilers and process heaters (i.e. Boiler MACT). This broad-reaching proposal could cost manufacturers more than $20 billion in compliance costs and place hundreds of thousands of jobs in jeopardy. Furthermore, as the NAM has communicated to the EPA, the proposed standards could almost never be achieved by any single, real-world source. In December 2010, the EPA asked the federal District Court for the District of Columbia for an extension to re-propose the rule, take industry comments and then finalize the package by April 2012. The court recently rejected this extension and the final rule is expected to be published by February 21, 2011. Unless Congress intervenes, we are likely to see a rule that neither the Administration nor industry wants finalized or implemented.

SEC/CFTC Derivatives Regulation

As end-users of over-the-counter (OTC) derivatives to manage risk, manufacturers in the United States have a strong interest in the implementation of the new rules on OTC derivatives in the Dodd-Frank Act. In drafting these regulations, we urge the Commodity Futures Trading Commission (CFTC) and the Securities and Exchange Commission (SEC) to avoid any new regulations on derivatives that could inadvertently harm economic growth. In particular, it is crucial that new regulations on derivatives include a strong and workable exemption for those end-users, like manufacturers, that use derivatives to hedge commercial risk. Rules that impose margin requirements on manufacturers or that impose financial regulation (such as a swap dealer or major swap participant) on non-financial businesses, could seriously harm the recovery by diverting companies' financial resources from much-needed business investment and job retention and creation. Similarly, regulations that make hedging too expensive will place manufacturers in the uncomfortable position of either having to divert additional money away from production or discontinue hedging business risk, which would require liabilities to reappear on corporate balance sheets, driving up the cost of capital.

SEC Special Disclosures Section 1502 (Conflict Minerals)

The Manufacturers support the underlying goal of Sec. 1502 to address the atrocities occurring in the Democratic Republic of Congo (DRC) and adjoining countries and are working with other stakeholders to help resolve the problem. We encourage the SEC to implement Sec. 1502 in a manner consistent with the realities of global supply chains and that acknowledges the facts on the ground in the DRC as well as the limited control downstream users have on the refiners/smelters and mines. A successful outcome is one that achieves the goals of the statute without unduly burdening legitimate trade. The NAM acknowledges the challenges involved with achieving this outcome and encourages the SEC to work with all affected industries to understand how the requirements can be realistically implemented across supply chains. The wrong path on this rulemaking could end up costing industries more than $11 billion to comply.

OSHA Injury and Illness Protection Program

OSHA is developing a new regulation that would mandate a standard for employers' safety and health programs, referred to as an Injury and Illness Prevention Program (I2P2). Such a concept is expected to be proposed in the spring of 2011 and would have a major impact on all aspects of both workplace safety enforcement and the promulgation of new regulations. We are concerned that this new proposal may not take into account the efforts by employers who already have effective safety and health programs in place or how this new mandate would disrupt safety programs that have achieved measurable successes. Based on preliminary information from OSHA, this proposal may allow OSHA investigators to substitute their judgment of the employer's plan on how to achieve compliance and whether some "injury" in the workplace should have been addressed in some way, even if these conditions were regulated under a specific standard or did not amount to a "significant risk" as required under the OSH Act.

Commerce/State/Defense Export Control Regulations

U.S. export control regulations have not been significantly revised since the Cold War. The result is a system that no longer fully protects our national security, has not kept up with accelerating technological change and does not function with the efficiency and transparency needed to keep the United States competitive in the global marketplace. The current regulations are eroding America's global technology leadership, harming the defense industrial base and costing U.S. jobs. Recent studies by the National Academies of Science and the Defense Science Board have concluded that the current export control regulations and system pose a threat to national security.

The Milken Institute estimates that if the export control regulations are modernized, U.S. high-tech exports could increase by $60 billion, resulting in 350,000 new jobs. Modernization will enhance the government's ability to protect national security interests while removing the burdens and disadvantages placed on U.S. high-technology manufacturers. The government should thoroughly modernize export controls to strengthen the industrial base, enhance national security and improve economic competitiveness. In this area, we applaud the Obama Administration for the steps it has taken thus far to modernize the export control system, but more is needed to improve the system in 2011 to protect manufacturing jobs.

DOT Transportation of Lithium Batteries Rulemaking

The Department of Transportation's (DOT) Pipeline and Hazardous Materials Safety Administration (PHMSA) proposed new shipping and handling requirements for the transportation of lithium ion and lithium metal batteries in January 2010. The rule mandates changes in the way lithium batteries and cells and products containing these batteries are transported in passenger and cargo aircraft. Of note, the PHMSA rejected all requests for extensions of the comment period and has severely limited industry input and technical discussions in what is an extremely complicated proposal, in the process creating serious inconsistencies between international and U.S. aviation regulations. The proposed rule applies to a variety of products and manufactured goods ranging from everyday consumer items to implantable medical devices. Billions of lithium batteries and products containing them are shipped annually by air without incident. The costs of the current proposal are conservatively estimated at $1 billion annually. If implemented as currently written, manufacturers will face reductions in existing air freight capacity, new costs associated with massive supply chain redesigns, additional training costs, inefficiencies that could cause confusion with international partners that adhere to alternate standards and lost business to foreign companies not subject to these proposed rules. Manufacturers strongly support a rule that instead achieves harmonization with internationally agreed-upon requirements for lithium battery transport.

DOT Hours of Service Rulemaking

The DOT's Federal Motor Carrier Safety Administration (FMCSA) has announced changes to the trucking hours of service rules first implemented in 2004. It has proposed to reduce well-established 11-hour driving and 14-hour on-duty times for truckers and to introduce new rest mandates. Over the past six years, driver and motor carrier safety performance has improved, and truck-involved fatalities and injuries have markedly declined. For manufacturers and those dependent on a healthy manufacturing economy, changes to the rule will have major impacts on distribution patterns, supply chains, justin-time delivery standards, trucking capacity and ultimately will add operational costs to be borne by shippers and motor carriers. In 2005, the American Trucking Association estimated that reducing the driving time by one hour and eliminating the 34-hour restart provision would cost affected industries more than $2 billion. While the DOT is adhering to the terms of a 2009 court negotiated settlement reached with Public Citizen by reviewing and reconsidering the 2008 Final Rule on Hours of Service, the Department is not obligated to alter the rule. The Department's recent public commentary on poor truck driver health and longevity is drawing some concern because the scientific data to justify a change in the current rule is not strong. Approximately 80 percent of the nation's freight by value moves by truck.

CPSC Product Safety Information Database

In 2008, Congress passed and the President signed the Consumer Product Safety Improvement Act (CPSIA), which, among other provisions, directed the Consumer Product Safety Commission (CPSC) to produce a product safety database that would provide consumers with a meaningful tool to research product safety information that is accurate and includes first-hand reports from consumers and public safety entities. Significant debate took place in Congress on the appropriate types of reporters to include in the database. The final CPSC rule, however, recognized that Congress provided an exhaustive list of reporters but strains credulity by expanding the definitions of consumers and public safety entities beyond their clear public meaning and the intent of the drafters of the legislation. The rule redefined the terms "consumer" to include trial attorneys and public safety entities to include "consumer advocacy organizations." As a result, the database could be filled with bogus reports inspired by political or financial motives rather than safety.

Congress also struck an appropriate balance between the speed of publication of reports and the desire for accuracy as well as the protection of confidential business information. The final rule provided for no such balance and creates a default for immediate publication before any meritorious claims regarding trade secrets or material inaccuracy are resolved. Once a trade secret is posted within a report, for example, no remedy is available to undo the damage. These claims as well as claims of inaccuracy, impossibility, or product misidentification must be resolved before the information is made public if the database is to provide helpful information to the public.

EXISTING RULES

The President has also promised a "look back" at existing rules to find those that are "outmoded, ineffective, insufficient, or excessively burdensome, and to modify, streamline, expand, or repeal them in accordance with what has been learned." We welcome an effort to streamline existing regulations and attempt to eliminate some of the accumulated burdens placed on manufacturing. But we fear that without proper oversight from Congress, this effort will be much like its predecessors – ineffective. Presidents since Jimmy Carter have required agencies to review their rules periodically, developed task forces to conduct the efforts, required plans from agencies and called for public nominations of rules for reform. But if the proper incentives do not exist or agencies are not held to account, then no measurable progress will be made. Since this Committee also oversees the federal workforce, perhaps it can consider having appropriate incentives included in federal employee performance appraisals to make these reviews effective. Additionally, future hearings on agency plans and their progress could help to make sure this effort produces results.

Manufacturers hope this is the dawn of a new regulatory era built on common sense with an understanding of the forces of global competition, the cumulative burden of existing rules and the needs of small business. We stand ready to assist in your efforts to help make the necessary improvements to our government.

Mr. Chairman, thank you for the opportunity to testify today, and I will be happy to respond to any questions.

Jay Timmons

Jay Timmons is president and CEO of the National Association of Manufacturers (NAM), the largest manufacturing association in the United States representing small and large manufacturers in every industrial sector. He became NAM president in January 2011.

Mr. Timmons is a leading advocate for the nearly 12 million Americans employed directly in manufacturing, educating the public and policy-makers on issues that affect this critical sector of the U.S. economy. He promotes a broad-based “Manufacturing Means Jobs!” agenda for maintaining U.S. competitiveness by lifting unnecessary burdens on manufacturing, including excessive taxation and regulation, the high cost of health care, expensive litigation and soaring energy costs.

He is driven by the principles instilled in him by his roots in the manufacturing town of Chillicothe, Ohio, where his grandfather worked at a Mead plant for nearly four decades and where he witnessed manufacturing’s ability to raise the quality of life for families and communities. Mr. Timmons' knowledge and expertise is valued and respected by influential policymakers on both sides of the aisle in Congress and the Administration. He knows how to navigate the complexities of the policymaking process in the nation’s capital and brings with him an exceptional understanding of manufacturing issues.

Prior to his appointment as NAM president, Mr. Timmons was executive vice president beginning in 2008. In 2005, he joined the NAM as senior vice president of policy and government relations.

His previous experience includes serving as chief of staff to Congressman, Governor and Senator George Allen (R-VA) from 1991 to 2002, and a term as executive director of the National Republican Senatorial Committee during the 2004 election cycle. When he first came to Washington in the 1980s, he served as press secretary to Congressman Jim Martin (R-NC) and later Alex McMillan (R-NC).

A passionate advocate for the adoption of companion animals, Mr. Timmons is a member of the Washington Humane Society Board of Directors and served as its chairman from 2006 to 2010. He is also a member of the Business Industry Political Action Committee (BIPAC) Executive Committee and the Board of Directors of Local Finance Solutions, Inc. He attended The Ohio State University and resides in McLean, Va.

Assessing Impediments of Job Creation
Editor: Joshua A. Lancolm
ISBN: 978-1-61324-352-7

Chapter 3

TESTIMONY OF HARRY C. ALFORD, NATIONAL BLACK CHAMBER OF COMMERCE (NBCC), BEFORE THE COMMITTEE ON OVERSIGHT & GOVERNMENT REFORM, HERAING ON "REGULATORY IMPEDIMENTS TO JOB CREATION"*

I would like to thank Chairman Issa and all the distinguished members of the committee for the opportunity to speak before you. On behalf of the National Black Chamber of Commerce and the 100,000 Black owned businesses that our organization represents, I thank you for your hard work and continued leadership. The topic of today's hearing, "Regulatory Impediments to Job Creation" is a matter of great importance and I applaud this committee for starting much needed dialogue on such an issue.

As we all know the administration, congress and the media have been debating how to get our economy back on track and spark sustainable job growth. As the economy begins to show signs of life we also recognize the fragile nature of our situation and understand that excessive constraints by the government can undermine the business sector and the entrepreneurial spirit of America.

---

* These remarks were delivered as testimony given before the Committee on Oversight and Government Reform on February 10, 2011. Harry C. Alford spoke on behalf of the National Black Chamber of Commerce (NBCC).

One of the most egregious burdens that I want to first mention is the Gulf moratorium imposed by the federal government as a result of the BP oil spill. With this moratorium the government has indicated that all U.S. energy companies will be lumped together and penalized for the actions of one company. As you know under this policy America's energy companies will not have the opportunity to buy new offshore drilling leases in the Gulf for the foreseeable future.

I have visited Louisiana and have talked with those who have been devastated by the spill; make no mistake I understand the environmental and economic damage caused by this tragic incident and I fully appreciate why the moratorium was initially put in place. Yet in the months following we have learned that this accident was caused by one bad actor in an otherwise responsible industry.

As we know too well, BP's safety record has been stained for many years and it's the responsibility of our government to appropriately address BP's long history of negligence. I have included with this testimony a graphic which clearly demonstrates the extent of BP's irresponsibility and lengthy record of safety violations. I think we can all acknowledge however that the government's actions should not punish those that follow the law, implement industry best practices and have demonstrated sterling safety records.

According to a study last year by Joseph R. Mason, PhD, the six-month offshore drilling moratorium cost the country $5 billion in economic activity and 19,500 jobs) The moratorium adds insult to injury and will prolong the economic damage seen in the Gulf. Now is the time to dust ourselves off and get back to work. We must learn from this incident and not be afraid to move forward with domestic energy production.

The longer we stall energy development, the longer the Gulf States will have to wait to create high paying jobs and benefit from new investment. The reality is we need jobs now. A moratorium will not help the American people or the American economy get moving again; rather, this policy decision will give foreign countries and foreign businesses a competitive advantage and prevent the advancements that will make our industries stronger.

Another area of overzealous regulation can be seen in the continued pursuit by the Environmental Protection Agency to impose greenhouse gas mandates. The EPA has gone beyond the intended scope of their authority and implemented far reaching policies by invoking the Clean Air Act (CAA) to defend their actions. This unprecedented expansion of power at the EPA is sending the wrong signals to the business community. According to the Senate report "EPA's Anti-Industrial Policy: Threatening Jobs and America's

Manufacturing Base" nearly 800,000 jobs are at risk due to EPA greenhouse gas proposals.[2]

Overreach by the agency has already created a maze of red tape for businesses both large and small. And it looks as if this regulation will not stop anytime soon; EPA Administrator Lisa Jackson recently reaffirmed that the administration continues to oppose any congressional plans that would curb the scope of the agency's greenhouse gas regulations.

The current state of EPA rulemaking will increase the financial burden on businesses and as we all know, limited resources translates into fewer jobs and higher prices for consumers. The impact will be especially hard on the energy sector and will disproportionately affect communities of color as African-American and Hispanic households spend a greater percentage of their income on energy. For many families in these communities higher energy prices creates some difficult choices between keeping the lights on and other expenses such as healthcare, food and housing.

Furthermore minority small businesses facing higher electricity and transportation costs are also feeling the pinch. This added financial strain can often result in small businesses cutting salaries, benefits and even jobs. It appears now is the time for Congress to lead and seriously consider a rollback of EPA's onerous regulations.

Reducing emissions to mitigate the effects of climate change is a very real challenge for the U.S. and the global community. There is no question we need to take proactive steps that will reduce our carbon footprint and make our environment cleaner. And yes we do need some reasonable regulations and a watchful eye from our government but the current onslaught of heavy business regulations is unsustainable, especially at a time when Washington looks to get our businesses back on track.

We must look to energy efficient technologies and cost-effective approaches to GHG reductions. Tapping into wind energy, clean burning energy sources such as natural gas and investing in cutting edge biofuels will play an important role to the long-term reductions in emissions. These are just a few technologies that our businesses communities are working on. It is these ideas that will allow our economy to prosper while also protecting our air and environment.

Throughout my career I have had the good fortune to work for several Fortune 100 companies. During this time I witnessed how the heavy hand of regulation can suppress business expansion and job growth. We must consider the financial impact of regulations on small and minority-owned businesses and we must transform America into a haven for free enterprise. Today I feel as though we are consistently squandering potential opportunities because of smothering regulations. According to the U.S. Department of Labor 13.9 million Americans are unemployed and for African Americans the unemployment rate stands at 16.5 percent.[3] I believe our business leaders are spending too much time, energy and resources dealing with regulatory burdens that restrict their business's ability to look forward and grow.

As I stated early, I thank the committee for starting this dialogue, I truly believe this discussion is vital to the decision making process of our leaders here in Washington and to the development of smart policies that will benefit all our American workers. I thank the members for their time and look forward to answering any of their questions.

President/CEO Harry C. Alford

In less than a decade, NBCC President/CEO and co-founder Harry C. Alford has established himself as perhaps the nation's preeminent champion of African American business empowerment. From a visionary concept of what Blacks need to do to fully seize their place in the economic mainstream, Mr. Alford has built a global organization that has earned a place at the table in the White House and at the top levels of Corporate America.

As the intellectual and spiritual linchpin of the NBCC, Mr. Alford has been responsible for opening doors that have led to billions of dollars in new business for Black owned firms throughout the nation. His courage and leadership have been noted by all in the rebuilding of the Gulf Coast in the aftermath of Hurricane Katrina. His relentless energy and advocacy is helping forge international business opportunities for African Americans and emerging entrepreneurs in Africa, the Caribbean, South America and the rest of the Black Diaspora. For this work he was formally named a Cultural Ambassador by the US State Department. A native of California, Mr. Alford has made his mark at the highest levels of both the private and public sectors. After earning top honors as Company Commander in the Army's Officer Candidate School class (0C3-72), Mr. Alford put his leadership skills to work in a series of key sales and executive positions at Fortune 100 companies such as Procter & Gamble, Johnson & Johnson and the Sara Lee Corporation. Mr. Alford has led large trade missions to Brazil, Ghana, Kenya and various nations in the Caribbean. Recently, he helped establish the French African Diaspora Chamber of Commerce in Paris, France. The birth and growth of the National Black Chamber of Commerce is consistent with the dynamic growth of

African American owned firms in the United States — the fastest growing segment in the nation per the US Census Bureau.

Mr. Alford is an award winning columnist for the National Newspaper Publishers Association and consults and speaks on business matters to groups and agencies throughout the nation. He proudly serves on the NNPA Foundation Board of Directors. He is an active member of the Board of Directors of the US Chamber of Commerce where he chairs the Regulatory Affairs Committee. He is a member of the 2008 Health Sector Assembly which is a think tank of national leaders concerned about healthcare. As a consultant, he has developed business models tailored to specific corporations and public agencies. Mr. Alford is regularly called upon by Congress to testify on various legislative initiatives related to small business development, the Gulf Coast rebuilding, e-commerce, healthcare, energy, tax reform and global trade issues. He received national recognition while delivering testimony concerning the current Cap and Trade Energy debate. Mr. and Mrs. Alford reside in Maryland and have two sons who were scholar athletes at the University of Maryland.

End Notes

[1] Dr. Joseph R. Mason, "Critique of the Inter-Agency Economic Report Estimating the Economic Effects of the Deepwater Drilling Moratorium on the Gulf Coast Economy", accessed at: http://www.saveusenergylobs.com/wpcontent/uploads/2010/09/Dr.-Mason-Critique-of-Administrations-Report.pdf

[2] U.S. Senate Environment and Public Works Report "EPA's Anti-Industrial Policy: Threatening Jobs and America's Manufacturing Base", September 28, 2010, accessed at: htto://epw.senate.gov/publichndex.cfm? FuseAction= Files.View&FileStore id=3ede3e93-813f-4449-97e6- 0d6eb54fbc9e

[3] U.S. Bureau of Labor Statistics (BLS), "Employment status of the civilian population by race, sex, and age", January 2011, accessed at: http://www.bis.gov/news.release/empsit.t02.htm

Assessing Impediments of Job Creation
Editor: Joshua A. Lancolm
ISBN: 978-1-61324-352-7

Chapter 4

TESTIMONY OF TOM NASSIF, PRESIDENT AND CEO OF WESTERN GROWERS, BEFORE THE COMMITTEE ON OVERSIGHT & GOVERNMENT REFORM, HEARING ON "REGULATORY IMPEDIMENTS TO JOB CREATION"*

Good Morning. Chairman Issa, Ranking Member Cummings and members of the committee, thank you for the opportunity to appear before you today. I am Tom Nassif, President and CEO of the Western Growers Association which is an agricultural trade association headquartered in Irvine, California. Western Growers members are small, medium and large-sized businesses who produce, pack and ship almost 90 percent of fresh fruits, nuts and vegetables grown in California and approximately 75 percent of the fresh fruits, nuts and vegetables grown in Arizona. In total, our members account for nearly half of the annual fresh produce grown in the United States, providing American consumers with healthy, nutritious food.

Studies demonstrate that every California agricultural job supports two jobs, and for every dollar our farmers and processors add to the agriculture sector, they are adding an additional $1.27 to the U.S. economy.

---

* These remarks were delivered as testimony given before the Committee on Oversight and Government Reform on February 10, 2011. Tom Nassif is President and CEO of Western Growers.

Nationwide, agriculture produces nearly $300 billion in value. Agriculture is the backbone of our economy, maintaining a safe and secure domestic food supply is not only a matter of national security but also of economic recovery. We are critical to job creation and community support.

We are also members of the very communities in which we grow, pack, and sell our products. Many of us are multi-generational, family farmers. We have a vested interest in sustaining the environment because we rely on the land and other natural resources to continue producing a safe and healthy crop. We have a responsibility to treat our employees with dignity and fairness, first because it's the right thing to do, and second, because without a reliable workforce, our products will rot in the field—our livelihoods and the livelihoods of our communities would disappear.

This morning, I will highlight some of the regulatory pressures that are making it increasingly difficult for us to continue to do our jobs—to do business in the United States. Let me be clear from the outset, we believe that compliance with laws and regulations is an important component of our social and environmental stewardship.

Yet, as you'll hear in my testimony, today we are experiencing a regulatory climate which is expensive. According to a recent CRS report, an estimated **$1** of every $9 of California farm capital investment goes toward regulatory compliance. Furthermore, these are dollars which are not being used to create additional jobs and economic activity. Beyond cost there are cases where regulatory requirements and restrictions are technically impossible to meet.

I would like to focus on two examples that are indicative of regulations that impact agriculture but which are advanced without valuable applied scientific knowledge, use of real world data, transparency and input from agricultural stakeholders. The result has been impractical controls, solutions and timelines that have severely impacted farmers.

INTERPRETATION OF THE ENDANGERED SPECIES ACT (ESA)

Situation

Current activity under the ESA threatens jobs supported by production agriculture. One of the more striking examples is the mariner in which the ESA has been implemented in the Sacramento-San Joaquin Delta.

California's water needs are largely met through the complex storage and conveyance systems of the federal Central Valley Project (CVP) and California's State Water Project (SWP). The two systems rely on two large water pumping facilities at the southern end of the Sacramento-San Joaquin Delta, where millions of acre feet of water move annually into the projects' twin aqueducts that convey water to cities and farms to the south.

Following litigation by environmental groups under the ESA alleging that the projects' operations harm the protected Delta smelt, federal agencies released a new biological opinion in late 2008 to govern operation of the pumps and protect the species.

The biological opinion (BiOp) developed by the U.S. Fish and Wildlife Service (FWS) relative to the protected Delta smelt was followed by another BiOp issued by the National Marine Fisheries Service (NMFS) relative to protected salmonids. Both BiOps were implemented under ESA-required "reasonable and prudent alternatives" (RPAs) developed by the agencies that severely restricted the operation of the pumps and greatly reduced the amount of water delivered to users in the south. The implementation of these ESA-driven restrictions coincided with one of the most severe droughts California has experienced in decades.

As a result, in 2009, only 10 percent of contractual allocations were delivered to CVP contractors, an all-time low. While the drought contributed to this reduction, water contracting agencies estimate that without the BiOp restrictions, the CVP allocation would have been three times higher (30 percent of contracted water). Water users successfully challenged the BiOps in federal court.

In May 2010, a federal judge issued an order barring NMFS from implementing two actions that restrict water exports from the CVP and SWP pumping plants in the south Delta. The court repeatedly criticized the federal agency's biological opinion and actions included in the reasonable and prudent alternative, characterizing portions of those documents as "unsupported by reasonable explanation," "simply indefensible," "inexplicable," and "not rational nor scientifically justified."

The judge also issued an order declaring unlawful several portions of the biological opinion and reasonable and prudent alternative prepared by the FWS to protect delta smelt. The Court held that under the National Environmental Policy Act, or NEPA, the federal government should have considered impacts on the human environment when implementing the pumping restrictions and that the specific restrictions imposed by the federal government were not "adequately justified by generally recognized scientific principles." A temporary plan will govern short-term Delta water operations while the agencies develop new BiOps.

Separately, in 2009, at the request of water users, members of Congress and the Administration, the National Academy of Sciences launched an independent study of the RPAs to determine whether they are scientifically valid and whether there are less economically damaging strategies for species protection. In March, 2010, the NAS panel issued a report that called into question the agencies' implementation of the BiOp RPAs, which had resulted in maximum water delivery reductions in most cases. While the panel found that restricting flows to the pumps is inherently "scientifically valid," in that *any* reduction of pumping operations certainly protects delta smelt and salmon smolts, it also stated:

"However, there is substantial uncertainty regarding the amount of flow that should trigger a reduction in exports. In other words, the specific choice of the negative flow threshold for initiating the RPA is less clearly supported by scientific analyses."

To the farmers and cities whose water is contractually delivered by the state and federal projects, this was confirmation that the federal fish agencies almost always selected the *most restrictive* response available rather than exercising the discretion available to them under the RPAs to mitigate water cutbacks.

Impact

The 2010 federal court decisions provide water users some hope for relief, as does the NAS report and, potentially, a second NAS report due later this year that will assess the impacts on protected fish species of the many other stressors, such as urban wastewater discharges, invasive and predatory non-native species, unscreened in-Delta water diversions, pesticide and other pollutant loading and other factors. Nonetheless, the damage caused by the implementation of the ESA in prior years cannot be undone. It includes, in 2009 alone, nearly 500,000 acres of farmland fallowed due to supply cutbacks and between $340 million and $370 million in economic harm. Estimated job losses vary widely, but there is no disagreement that the number of lost jobs runs in the thousands in this already-economically stressed region. Several San Joaquin Valley farm communities suffered unemployment of 40 percent or higher.

Solution

The solution is not to compel regulated communities to turn to the courts in costly and divisive litigation. Instead, as the court held in this matter, the agencies responsible for implementing the ESA should also comply with NEPA, which will require not only protecting endangered species but also considering and mitigating the human and economic impact of their regulatory decisions.

Accordingly, we are seeking an amendment to the ESA that would strengthen transparency through improved interagency coordination and consultation with potentially impacted stakeholders early in the process of developing RPAs.

An amendment to the ESA could provide a way forward that protects threatened and endangered species while minimizing economic impacts to humans and ultimately restoring the credibility of the ESA and the agencies charged with its implementation.

In addition, we ask the Committee to investigate how the Departments and agencies with the authority and responsibility to implement the ESA have modified their agency culture in light of recent, relevant court decisions and in this case, the findings of the National Academy, to avoid repeating the same flawed procedures.

H-2A Regulations Situation

In the absence of immigration reform, the II-2A or temporary agricultural guest-worker visa program is specialty crop agriculture's only option to acquire with certainty the legal labor force necessary to harvest America's fruits and vegetables. Studies demonstrate that domestically-born workers are unwilling to work in America's specialty crop fields.

The regulations governing the H-2A program have been dramatically altered three times in the last three years. The program suffers crucial flaws including inconsistent interpretations of the Department of Labor (DOL) regulations by DOL employees and an institutional hostility towards agricultural labor programs. As a result agricultural employers are punished for using the only option we have to hire a legal workforce. Moreover, DOL' s actions are actually undermining the objectives of the Department of Homeland Security.

Impact

While the examples of administrative challenges are numerous, the three egregious examples below highlight problems that should be easily resolved.

- DOL's Chicago Processing Center (CPC) is unresponsive to user concerns and questions, and delays in processing proper H-2A applications are common. It is impossible to contact a live person at the CPC to inquire about a pending H-2A application and Employment and Training Administration staff have refused our requests to allocate a staff person to answer phone calls from H-2A users. While there is an e-mail address devoted to this purpose, questions often go unanswered.
- In addition, we have members who have submitted clean applications but received no response from the CPC for several months and only just before the employer's date of need for workers to harvest the crop. Only after repeated inquiry from our Association and various Members of Congress intervening did the CPC respond. Moreover, it is common for CPC's attorneys to reverse its adverse interpretation after an employer appeals the determination, rendering the appeal moot. However, by the time the application is approved, the employer does not get the workers until several weeks after the date of need, resulting in adverse financial impact.
- The current regulations require filing of the application, recruitment, and securing of housing 60-75 days before date of need. However, it is difficult to predict labor needs and project the

availability of recruited domestic workers so far in advance of the date of need. While DOL has ample time to certify an H-2A application (i.e., to make a determination that U.S. workers will not be adversely impacted by bringing in H-2A foreign workers and that the H-2A employer intends to comply with the program's requirements), the Department is still routinely delaying certifications and is slow to respond to questions and concerns.

- Agricultural employers that use the H-2A program often utilize multiple job classifications — some are H-2A while others are not H-2A. Fulltime, year round workers are not eligible for the H-2A program, since H-2A applications are granted only for temporary or seasonal work. The DOL has determined that any work performed by non-H-2A employees that is also performed by H-2A employees is to be considered "corresponding employment." As such, the non-H2A employees are entitled to all benefits provided to H-2A employees including payment of the elevated wage rates of the H-2A program, free housing and inbound and out-bound transportation. For example, if an employer has a crew of cabbage harvest workers who are H-2A visa holders, no other person on the farm can perform any cabbage harvesting work, even if the worker is a foreman providing instruction on harvesting, or the harvesting work being performed is incidental to the employee's primary occupation. If an employee is not primarily performing cabbage harvesting work, incidental cabbage harvesting work should not propel the employee into the H-2A job classification. This overbroad definition of "corresponding employment" creates further uncertainty, difficulty in planning, and financial loss.
- The DOL's Wage & Hour Division (WHD) is currently assessing H-2A employers hundreds of thousands of dollars in fines and backpay for technical compliance violations of the H-2A program. For example, WHD recently audited an H-2A employer and found they unwittingly failed to report the involuntary and voluntary separation of domestic workers to the CPC and/or state workforce agency. WHD assessed a fine of $1,000.00 per worker; plus $1,000 per worker for failure to pay the three-fourths guarantee (even though it is undisputed these workers were properly terminated or voluntarily quit); plus the three-fourths guarantee for hours not worked and wages not earned. Based on 56 domestic workers, the total fines and backpay levied was over $475,000.00. Another H-

2A employer who otherwise did everything correctly did not understand that the number of hours offered (not just worked) during the pay period is now required by regulation to appear on an employee's paystub.

- For this technical violation, the employer was assessed fines of nearly $500,000.00. In neither case were workers, domestic or foreign, found to be mistreated, or otherwise denied the wages, benefits or conditions set forth in the regulations. Unfortunately, the H-2A rules are so complicated, it's virtually impossible for an employer not to commit some technical violation, which could lead to financial ruin.

The financial harm caused by DOL's delays, and inconsistent interpretations, and overly punitive enforcement strategy has resulted in confusion, frustration, and pecuniary loss by employers struggling to use the program.

Oversight of DOL's management of the H-2A visa program is vital to ensuring the program runs as smoothly as possible. There is no other recourse for the specialty crop industry to address its need for labor. Yet, our substantive comments to inform the rulemaking process were disregarded by DOL.

At public meetings held by DOL officials to "explain" the current iteration of the rules and Agency resulting interpretations of the regulation, it was clear that DOL is instructing its employees to focus not on making the regulations operational but rather to focus on enforcement of unworkable regulations. As a result there is extreme concern among the H-2A usesr community about the DOL's systemic hostility towards and abuses against H-2A employers. Even longtime users have begun to abandon the 11-2A program because of the risk that minor technical violations discovered during a DOL audit will result in fines and penalties that may lead to financial devastation.

Solution

Precious DOL staff resources are increasingly being devoted to audits and exacting of fines rather than seeking meaningful solutions to improve the dysfunctional visa program. We respectfully request this Committee use its oversight authority to examine DOL's administration of this visa program culminating in a report authored by DOL to this Committee explaining its decisions and rationale concerning issues such as: staff allocation, interpretations of the H-2A regulations, delays and inconsistency in its certification process, and assessments of fines and penalties for technical violations that are financially ruinous for family farmers.

Let me be clear, even if the DOL were to magically correct all issues related to the H-2A program tomorrow, it would not solve agriculture's labor crisis. We still need immigration reform legislation tailored for agriculture to deal with our existing experienced workforce, who are not currently eligible for the H-2A program. Moreover, the infrastructure is not in place for most agricultural employers to access the H-2A program, which is why H-2A users make up only 2-4% of the agricultural labor workforce. However, for those employers who choose or are compelled to use the H-2A program now, immediately correcting the systemic problems with H-2A is critical. Without improvements to this program and the manner in which it is implemented by DOL, United States agricultural and specialty crop production in particular will continue to suffer unnecessary financial loss due to product being left to rot in the field because our farmers lack the labor they need and requested to get their food to consumers in America and around the world.

Conclusion

On behalf of American specialty crop agriculture we are appreciative of this Committee's willingness to examine the myriad of regulations American producers are forced to navigate in an attempt to continue to cultivate this great land of ours. The impact of the costs, job losses and competitive disadvantage for U.S. Specialty Crop production created by this regulatory environment is perhaps best brought home as follows:

I have members who have moved portions of their operations out of the United States, not because the cost of getting product to market is less in other countries, but because regulatory uncertainty is mitigated and there are local populations able and willing to work harvesting specialty crops.

Specialty crop producers in the United States today are subject to a variety of social responsibility audits, which include labor, conservation, environmental and food safety requirements. They are not moving production from the United States to avoid responsible business practices. They face these in other countries too, particularly if they want to sell to the United States. They are leaving because many regulations are not about common sense responsibility, but about compliance with an agency's' interpretation of the law regardless of the real world impact, available science and options for workable compliance.

Western Growers appreciates the Committee's willingness to listen to our concerns and looks forward to working with you to do something about them.

Assessing Impediments of Job Creation
Editor: Joshua A. Lancolm
ISBN: 978-1-61324-352-7

Chapter 5

TESTIMONY OF MICHAEL J. FREDRICH, PRESIDENT, MCM COMPOSITES, LLC, MANITOWOC, WISCONSIN, BEFORE THE COMMITTEE ON OVERSIGHT & GOVERNMENT REFORM, HEARING ON "REGULATORY IMPEDIMENTS TO JOB CREATION"*

Chairman Issa and Ranking Member Cummings, thank you for inviting me to testify today. My name is Michael Fredrich, President of MCM Composites, LLC (MCM) located in Manitowoc, Wisconsin. MCM Composites is a privately held company with 60 non-union employees. We are located on the Lake Michigan shoreline 50 miles north of Milwaukee. MCM is a custom thermoset molder of parts ranging from handles for high-end cookware to emergency oxygen system containers for the Boeing 787 (the Boeing 787 is the first composite commercial aircraft). A thermoset composite is a type of plastic which has physical properties which are required in applications that require resistance to heat, exposure to hydrocarbons, electrical conductivity, and compressive force.

---

* These remarks were delivered as testimony given before the Committee on Oversight and Government Reform on February 10, 2011. Michael J. Fredrich is President of MCM Composites, LLC.

Economic Gravity

Gravitational force is omnipresent. It goes virtually unnoticed but over time it will compress your spine. Government regulations act on the economy much the same as gravitational force acts on an object -- it burdens our economic system and eventually will compress our economy.

Estimates of the cost of federal regulations range from $ 1 trillion (Heritage Foundation) to $1.75 trillion (Small Business Administration) per year. This represents around 7% of our annual GDP. Burdensome regulations are a stealth tax on every person in this country. The cost of regulation incurred by all businesses is eventually passed on to the consumer and our workforce. Regulatory costs require business owners like me to devote more time and resources to government compliance, which means less capital devoted to investment and job creation.

Macro View

Our country has experienced a steady erosion of manufacturing jobs. Our import of products greatly exceeds our exports. For our country to reverse this trend we must be able to compete globally and this can only be accomplished through productivity and low burden costs. We cannot compete on labor costs. The average hourly wage in China is $1.36 (BLS 2008) and in India it is $0.91 (BLS 2005).

The total cost of production labor (hourly wage plus health care, payroll taxes, unemployment compensation, etc) in China, India, East Asia, and Mexico is only a fraction of the cost in the US. What costs $30 per hour to produce in the US costs $15 per hour in East Asia and $5.00 in Mexico. The only way we can compete -- *and we can compete* -- in the world economy is through higher productivity coupled with lower overhead burden. The current burden includes the compliance costs of federal regulations, and with the threat of additional burden the U.S. is moving entirely in the wrong direction.

A $1 trillion annual regulatory burden is taking its toll on U.S. competitiveness – on my ability to compete. Fifty federal agencies and 150,000 pages of rules is enough.

Front Line View (of Our Free Market System)

Our company competes in the world economy. We ship product to Germany, Canada, China, Mexico, Dominican Republic, and Puerto Rico. We can compete with manufactures in these countries and within our own country because we provide value --which is not always the lowest price. Our value flows from engineering expertise, investment in capital equipment and a productive workforce -- all coupled with the lowest overhead burden we can achieve. Therein is the issue: anything that increases our burden (costly federal regulations) diminishes our ability to compete by increasing our costs.

The trend is not good. There is an attempt to govern through federal agency regulations initiatives which would never pass Congress.

Currently being considered are regulations that will add to the to the already high regulatory burden placed on private sector businesses, to wit;

Patient Protection and Affordable Care Act

- 1099 requirement and paperwork burden. Our company deals with approximately 375 different vendors. This year we issued 11 1099 forms. It took 3 hours to assemble the information and type the forms. It would take 2 weeks to prepare 1099's for all of our vendors. This requirement, which had no place whatsoever in the health care bill, will add $2,400 (80 hrs @ $30 per hour) to our regulatory burden. My business will also be required to report employee health care premiums to the government, and eventually prove that it provides government-approved insurance (if we decide, or can continue to afford insurance).
- Employer Mandates and Regulations Impeding Choice and Affordability. We offer a high deductable HSA health care plan to our employees. It is a good plan because it introduces market incentives to a system that has been corrupted by a 3rd party payment system. It encourages preventative care by paying 100% (no deductable) for such things as physicals, mammograms, and colonoscopies. The total monthly premium is $1,050 of which we pay 70% and our employees pay 30%. The thought of an unelected bureaucrat deciding the type of insurance we provide is abhorrent. Undoubtedly our plan will not meet with bureaucratic approval and we will be forced to change, if we can afford to, or drop coverage

and pay the fine. We are between Scylla and Charybdis. Either choice will raise our regulatory burden.

- Medicare Payroll Tax. Starting in 2013, individuals with incomes over $200,000 will see their Medicare payroll taxes increase. Most privately owned businesses are structured as Sub-S or LLC corporations. The income of the business is passed to the ownership in the form of a schedule "C" or K-1 and the tax is paid at the individual level. This is a tax increase on small business. It raises our regulatory burden and takes away more of my capital that can be used for investment, pay increases or new jobs.

Injury and Illness Preventative Program—OSHA

This is nothing more than a "prove yourself innocent" plan and it is a waste of time and money. The free market is providing all the necessary incentives. All businesses are required to carry worker's compensation insurance which covers work related injuries. The cost of this insurance is a function of the number and severity of the claims. Our monthly premium for this insurance is $4,500. We can get a rebate of up to 40% if we do not have a claim so we have a strong incentive to provide a safe workplace environment which morally we would do regardless of the monetary incentive.

Our company has a safety committee comprised of people working in every area of our facility. They meet monthly and inspect the plant for potential safety issues. All findings are fixed immediately. We also have a monthly cash incentive payment of up to $15 per person if we are injury free.

We have a system and it works. It is efficient. We do not need more burdensome regulation to mirror what we are already doing. Engaging my employees in additional government-required activities rather than focusing on their jobs will decrease productivity, and make us less able to compete and win business. Jobs will be lost or not created at MCM Composites, LLC.

EPA Regulation

This agency needs to be regulated. All existing regulations must be reviewed and all pending regulations must be stopped. The potential damage is pervasive so I will focus on one element -- the effect of proposed regulations on the cost of electricity.

The majority of our nation's electricity output is fueled by fossil fuel - - coal, oil and natural gas. Unless we move toward terrestrial energy (nuclear power) it will remain so. We can cover every square mile of this country with wind mills and solar panels and it would not meet our energy needs so forget about it. The problem with wind and solar is lack of energy density and no EPA regulation will change that physical reality.

Our company is a large consumer of electricity. Behind labor (12% of our cost structure) and raw material (40%) electricity represents around 7% of our total operating costs. Our monthly bill averages $22,000.

Most of the electricity we use is generated by a coal-fired power plant. Enhanced EPA regulations increasing the cost of producing electricity using coal will be passed on directly to our company and added to our regulatory burden and make it more difficult for us to compete in the world market. Rising energy costs mean fewer jobs added at MCM Composites, LLC.

SUMMARY

The cost of regulation is cumulative and pervasive. The cost of every product and service we buy includes some regulatory burden. We in turn include this cost in the selling price of our product which must cover our production cost, interest on our debt, and provide a profit. And yes, I can proudly state that our goal is to make the highest profit the free market will allow. If regulatory burden continues to grow we, along with all other private sector companies, will no longer be able to compete in the world market. Jobs will not be created and new businesses will not be formed. You will suffocate the system that has produced everything we enjoy today. It is that simple.

Thank you. I look forward to your questions.

Assessing Impediments of Job Creation
Editor: Joshua A. Lancolm
ISBN: 978-1-61324-352-7

Chapter 6

TESTIMONY OF JACK BUSCHUR, BUSCHUR ELECTRIC, BEFORE THE COMMITTEE ON OVERSIGHT & GOVERNMENT REFORM, HEARING ON "REGULATORY IMPEDIMENTS TO JOB CREATION"*

Good morning Chairman Issa, and members of the Committee. I would like to thank you for giving me the opportunity to speak with you today regarding the impact that regulations have had on small businesses.

I am the owner of Buschur Electric, a small electric contracting business in Minster, Ohio. We currently have 18 employees, down from 30 employees in 2009. My business works on commercial, industrial, institutional and residential properties.

There are three specific regulatory issues I want to bring to the committee's attention today – the EPA Lead RRP rule, Project Labor Agreements, and prevailing wage rules. All three of these regulatory burdens have had a negative impact on small businesses and our ability to create new jobs.

In 2008, EPA finalized a rule requiring firms to be certified, and their employees trained, on lead safe practices during home renovations on homes built before 1978. Originally, the rule allowed homeowners to opt out of these requirements if they signed a waiver confirming that there were no pregnant

* These remarks were delivered as testimony given before the Committee on Oversight and Government Reform on behalf of the National Federation of Independent Business (NFIB) on February 10, 2011. Jack Buschur is President of Buschur Electric.

women or children six and under living in the home. In the weeks leading up to the rule's effective date, in April 2010, many NFIB members contacted the organization expressing alarm that they had just heard about the rule or its requirements. Members said that they had difficulty getting their employees into EPA-compliant training classes, and some reported having to pay excessive costs to enroll in compliance classes before the deadline due to the heavy demand.

EPA eventually revoked its opt-out rule, requiring all home renovations in pre-1978 homes to follow lead-safe practices, thus increasing the cost of renovations for homeowners that had no at-risk individuals. Such inflexible standards have the effect of driving down demand for renovation services. Or worse, homeowners could seek to have renovations performed by unlicensed, underground contractors, which increases the safety risk to everyone.

I have found this situation to be a prime example of a regulation that hinders my ability as a small business owner to add jobs and help get our economy growing again. I first found out about this burdensome rule at a recent project. An inspector from the Occupational Safety and Health Administration informed the project's general contractor that all subcontractors were required to have "on the job training" in order to be in compliance with the RRP Rule. I had to have two of my employees go through a seven hour certified training course on site. In addition, the general contractor had to make arrangements such as Lead Air Sample Analysis, OSHA Lead Awareness training, Pre Assumed Lead Exposure Blood Panel, Post Assumed Lead Exposure Blood Panel, Respirator Clearance Exam, Respirator Fit Exam, Medical Exam for each employee, the purchase of the necessary PPE gear and Lead Assessment by a certified professional (the lead assessment alone was $1,260.00 per day for 3 days). The overall cost for the general was about $10,000. We eventually learned that we in fact did not need to be certified or trained to do the work because the concentration of lead dust at the worksite was not high enough to pose a risk to anyone.

As I witnessed the amount of time and money the general contractor exhausted in an effort to be compliant, I decided that my business would not become an RRP-compliant company. I expect many other similar companies will not either. The expenses are outrageous, the amount of paperwork is far too burdensome, and the exposure to liability is too great for my business to take on.

I believe that the RRP rule is a perfect example of a regulation that will limit competitive bidding on projects and increases the cost of projects to property owners and taxpayers.

I am also very concerned about two labor regulations that also adversely impact small business – Project Labor Agreements (PLAs) and prevailing wage. The federal government's insistence on PLAs makes it much more difficult for a business like mine to bid on projects. Typical PLAs are pre-hire contracts that require projects be awarded only to contractors and subcontractors that agree to:

- Recognize unions as the representatives of their employees on that job
- Use the union hiring hall to obtain workers
- Obtain apprentices exclusively from union apprenticeship programs
- Pay into union benefit plans
- Obey costly, restrictive and inefficient work rules

The use of Project Labor Agreements is a discriminatory tactic that prevents non-union construction companies from working on government construction projects. The U.S. Department of Labor's Bureau of Labor Statistics found in their annual report on union membership that from 2009 to 2010 union membership fell from 14.5 percent to 13.1 percent of the U.S. private construction work force. By preventing 86.9 percent of construction companies from bidding, PLAs increase the cost of construction by unfairly reducing the number of companies which can competitively bid. When you consider the fact that the construction industry currently has an unemployment rate of over 20 percent, it makes no sense to impose PLAs or other regulations that serve as impediments to job creation.

We have not been directly affected by PLAs over the last couple years, as the projects have been either too large or too far out of our area. However, I am very concerned that if a right-sized project with a PLA does come up for bid in our area, we will be unable to compete for the work., making it even harder for our company to get back on its economic feet.

Another area that has an adverse impact on small business job creation is the prevailing wage rules. With the slow economy the last couple of years, we have been forced to perform prevailing wage work in order to survive. These projects (we currently have 7 prevailing wage projects) create a lot of additional record keeping that must be sent to the prevailing wage coordinator, along with additional copies to the Division of Industrial Compliance and Labor, for when the unions file an audit request after the job is complete.

At the time a prevailing wage project is awarded, my firm has to issue employee notification forms to employees on the job, advising the wage rate and applicable fringe benefits paid per hour. Then, every week we have to do the following:

- Review prevailing wage updates and prepare updated employee notification forms to all employees working on the job.
- Print and review certified payroll reports for each prevailing wage job.
- Compile applicable spreadsheet, per project, for payment of training fringe benefits to certified training program.
- Compile applicable spreadsheet, per project, for payment of fringe benefits to certified retirement plan.
- Compile applicable spreadsheet for tracking of all prevailing wage hours worked per job, and all prevailing wage fringe benefits due per job, all to prepare for the possibility of a prevailing wage audit.

Then, every month, we must:

- Submit certified payroll reports to the prevailing wage coordinator for each project.
- Submit payment of training account fringe benefits to certified training program
- Submit payment of fringe benefits to certified retirement plan.

I thank you for the opportunity to share my concerns with you, and I urge the committee to take a hard look at how the regulatory environment can stifle small business job creation and growth.

Assessing Impediments of Job Creation
Editor: Joshua A. Lancolm
ISBN: 978-1-61324-352-7

Chapter 7

TESTIMONY OF JAMES GATTUSO, SENIOR RESEARCH FELLOW IN REGULATORY POLICY, THE HERITAGE FOUNDATION, BEFORE THE COMMITTEE ON OVERSIGHT & GOVERNMENT REFORM, HEARING ON "REGULATORY IMPEDIMENTS TO JOB CREATION"*

Chairman Issa and members of the Committee, thank you for the opportunity to testify today on this important topic.

My name is James Gattuso. I am a Senior Research Fellow in Regulatory Policy at The Heritage Foundation. The views I express in this testimony are my own, and should not be construed as representing any official position of The Heritage Foundation.

> The American people deserve a regulatory system that works for them, not against them: a regulatory system that protects and improves their health, safety, environment, and well-being and improves the performance of the economy without imposing unacceptable or unreasonable costs on society; regulatory policies that recognize that the private sector and private markets are the best engine for economic

* These remarks were delivered as testimony given before the Committee on Oversight and Government Reform on February 10, 2011. James Gattuso is Senior Research Fellow in Regulatory Policy of The Heritage Foundation.

> growth; regulatory approaches that respect the role of State, local, and tribal governments; and regulations that are effective, consistent, sensible, and understandable. We do not have such a regulatory system today.

This strong and concise description of sound regulatory policy is from Executive Order 12866, issued by President Bill Clinton in 1993. And his conclusion that the regulatory system falls short of what's best for the nation is even truer today than it was 18 years ago.

From the lighting in their homes, to the volume of their television sets, to the cars they buy, Americans are facing an unprecedented tide of red tape that is increasing prices, reducing innovation, and destroying jobs.

The impact of this regulation is difficult to measure precisely. Unlike direct spending, regulatory burdens imposed on businesses and consumers appear in no budget and are recorded in no ledger. However, by any reckoning, the burden is substantial and growing. This growth is not confined to one administration or political party. In fact, according to the Office of Management and Budget, regulatory costs have grown every year since 1981. The last several years of the George W. Bush administration were particularly busy ones in terms of regulatory activity.

Last year, however, the number and cost of new regulations imposed by federal agencies reached unprecedented levels. Based upon reports from the Government Accountability Office, in fiscal year 2010 alone some 43 major new rules increasing regulatory burdens were issued by federal agencies. The total annual cost for these rules, based on estimates by the regulators themselves, tops $26.5 billion, the highest level since at least 1981, the earliest date for which figures are available.[1]

Fifteen of the 43 major rules issued during the fiscal year involve financial regulation. Another five stem from the Patient Protection and Affordable Care Act adopted by Congress in early 2010. Ten others come from the Environmental Protection Agency, including the first mandatory reporting of "greenhouse gas" emissions and $10.8 billion in new automotive fuel economy standards (adopted jointly with the National Highway Traffic Safety Administration).

It should be noted that the actual cost of regulations adopted in FY 2010 is almost certainly much higher than $26.5 billion annually. As a first matter, the cost of non-economically significant rules—rules deemed not likely to have an annual impact of $100 million or more—is not calculated by agencies. Moreover, regulatory agencies did not quantify costs for 12 of the 43 economically significant rules adopted in FY 2010.

Many more are on the way. According to one estimate, the financial regulation legislation recently adopted by Congress will alone require 243 new formal rulemakings by 11 different federal agencies.[2]

A similarly large number of rulemakings will likely be required to implement the new health care law. Significant new regulation is also in the pipeline at EPA, as well as at independent agencies such as the Federal Communications Commission and the Consumer Product Safety Commission.

Overall, the latest Unified Agenda released by OMB shows that regulatory agencies have 183 more regulations in the pipeline now than they did last year, 40 of which are "economically significant"—an increase of 20 percent.[3]

The types of costs imposed by these rules vary as much as the regulations themselves. One of the most significant is the effect on jobs. A pending EPA rule on boilers, for example, threatens some 71,000 jobs related to the paper and pulp industry alone.[4] "Net neutrality" rules by the FCC is forecast to reduce employment by hundreds of thousands of jobs.[5] A recent report by the Manufacturer's Alliance projected the loss of 7.3 million jobs by 2020 from the EPA's proposed ozone rule.[6]

These figures show only part of the jobs picture, however. Economic studies can only capture effects on existing industries and technologies. The dogs that don't bark are not counted: new technologies that are stunted, new products that are never brought to market, and ideas that are never acted upon.

Regulations can create jobs as well as eliminate them. But this is not always a good thing. For instance, a new regulation can—and in fact usually does—create more demand for lawyers, lobbyists, and even regulators themselves. Few, however, would consider this a good thing. For the same reason, policymakers should be wary of claims about new rules creating "green jobs." If those jobs are based on artificial mandates or restrictions that are not otherwise justified, they add nothing to overall prosperity.

In the long run, total employment levels will likely be relatively constant. As the economy adjusts—according to most economists—total employment will trend toward a stable level. But to an individual American out of a job, news that in a few years the economy will achieve equilibrium may not provide much consolation. And even after that long-term leveling of employment is reached, total income and prosperity in the economy remains lower than it would otherwise be.

It is critical that policymakers increase scrutiny of new and existing rules to ensure that each is necessary and that costs are minimized. President Obama has already taken an important first step toward reform, issuing an Executive Order reiterating the obligation of regulatory agencies to carefully review new regulations and to review rules already on the books. This is a welcome step. At the same time, however, I am concerned that the initiative falls short of what is needed. For instance, although President Obama has stated that he has called for a "government-wide review" of existing rules, agencies only are required to submit preliminary plans for ongoing reviews in the future. This adds little to the review requirements that already exist in statute and prior executive orders. Moreover, President Obama's order excludes independent agencies, thus exempting some of the biggest sources of regulation.

Mr. Chairman, I would like to commend you for initiating your review of regulation by requesting input directly from over 150 research organizations and individuals,[7] as well as American businesses—who have had first-hand experience with the real burdens of regulation. Supplemented by information provided via your new website— americanjobcreators.com— your efforts promise to provide vital information as to what is and is not working in our regulatory system, as well as focus attention on this vital issue.

There are a number of legislative steps Congress can take in order to ensure proper scrutiny of new and existing rules. Among these:

1. Require Congressional Approval of Major Regulations that Place New Burdens on the Private Sector

Under the 1996 Congressional Review Act, Congress has the means to veto new regulations from agencies. To date, however, that authority has been used successfully only once. Under legislation introduced in the House by Congressman Geoff Davis (H.R. 10) and in the Senate by Senator Rand Paul (S. 299), the review process would be strengthened by requiring congressional approval before any major regulation takes effect. Such a system would ensure a congressional check on regulators, as well as ensure the accountability of Congress itself.

2. Require a Cost Analysis of All Legislation Imposing New Regulatory Burdens

Although all proposed legislation must be scored by the Congressional Budget Office to determine likely fiscal costs, there is no similar requirement for scoring regulatory costs. Members should not be asked to vote on proposals without the best possible estimate of likely costs. All bills proposing new or expanded regulation should undergo a regulatory impact analysis analyzing and quantifying (where possible) the likely costs and benefits. This "regulatory scoring" would ideally be performed by a new "Congressional

Regulation Office," similar to the Congressional Budget Office. Such a step could be taken by Congress on its own initiative and without presidential approval.

Establish a Sunset Sate for New Federal Regulations

Once adopted, rules tend to be left in place, even if they have outlived their usefulness. Currently, under section 610 of the Regulatory Flexibility Act, rules that have a substantial effect on a significant number of small entities must be reviewed by the promulgating agency every 10 years. In practice, however, such review, if it occurs at all, is usually performed in a cursory manner. To ensure that substantive review occurs, regulations should automatically expire if not explicitly reaffirmed. This requirement should be applied to all rules, not just those affecting small businesses. Such "sunset" dates should also be included in legislation imposing new regulation.

CONCLUSION

While reforming the regulatory process is important, it is also important to note that such reforms will not by themselves solve the problem of overregulation. No set of procedural reforms will be enough to stem the regulatory tide. Ultimately, regulatory burdens will rise until policymakers fully appreciate the burdens that regulations impose on Americans, and exercise the political will necessary to limit and reduce those burdens. I hope today's hearing serves as one step towards that end.

* * *

The Heritage Foundation is a public policy, research, and educational organization operating under Section 501(c)(3). It is privately supported and receives no funds from any government at any level, nor does it perform any government or other contract work.

The Heritage Foundation is the most broadly supported think tank in the United States. During 2009, it had 581,000 individual, foundation, and corporate supporters representing every state in the U.S. Its 2009 income came from the following sources:

Individuals 80%, Foundations 17%, Corporations 3%

The top five corporate givers provided The Heritage Foundation with 1.6% of its 2009 income. The Heritage Foundation's books are audited annually by the national accounting firm of McGladrey & Pullen. A list of major donors is available from The Heritage Foundation upon request.

Members of The Heritage Foundation staff testify as individuals discussing their own independent research. The views expressed are their own and do not reflect an institutional position for The Heritage Foundation or its board of trustees.

End Notes

[1] See James L. Gattuso, Diane Katz, and Stephen A. Keen, "Red Tape Rising: Obama's Torrent of New Regulation," Heritage Foundation *Backgrounder* No. 2482, October 26, 2010.

[2] Davis Polk, "Summary of the Dodd–Frank Wall Street Reform and Consumer Protection Act, Enacted into Law on July 21, 2010," Davis Polk & Wardwell, LLP, July 21, 2010.

[3] Susan Dudley, "An Ambitious Regulatory Agenda," George Washington University Regulatory Studies Center, *Regulatory Policy Commentary,* December 24, 2010, at *http://www.regulatorystudies.gwu.edu/ images/commentary/20101224_dudley_regulatory_agenda.pdf.*

[4] Fisher International, "Economic Impact of Pending Air Regulations on the U.S. Pulp and Paper Industry," August 2010, at *http://www.afandpa.org/pressreleases.aspx?id=1545.*

[5] Charles M. Davidson and Bret T. Swanson, "Net Neutrality, Investment & Jobs: Assessing the Potential Impacts of the FCC's Proposed Net Neutrality Rules on the Broadband Ecosystem," Advanced Communications Policy and Law Institute, New York University, June 2010.

[6] Donald A. Norman, "Economic Implications of EPA's Proposed Ozone Standard," Manufacturer's Alliance Economic Report, September 2010.

[7] In response to your request, my colleague Diana Katz and I identified 20 specific regulations which we believe should be eliminated, ranging from the individual mandate for health insurance to new FCC regulation of Internet service providers. These recommendations have also been detailed in a Heritage research report issued last month. See Diane Katz, "Rolling Back Red Tape: 20 Regulations to Eliminate," Heritage Foundation *Backgrounder* No. 2510, January 26, 2011, at http://www.heritage.org/Research/Reports/2011/01/Rolling-Back-Red-Tape-20-Regulations-to-Eliminate.

Assessing Impediments of Job Creation
Editor: Joshua A. Lancolm
ISBN: 978-1-61324-3

Chapter 8

TESTIMONY OF KAREN KERRIGAN, PRESIDENT & CEO, SMALL BUSINESS AND ENTREPRENEURSHIP COUNCIL, BEFORE THE COMMITTEE ON OVERSIGHT & GOVERNMENT REFORM, HEARING ON "REGULATORY IMPEDIMENTS TO JOB CREATION"*

Chairman Issa and Ranking Member Cummings, the Small Business & Entrepreneurship Council (SBE Council) is pleased to provide testimony today regarding regulatory impediments to job creation. Our nation's small business owners and entrepreneurs are especially impacted by the burden and cost of regulation, and we are pleased that both Congress and the White House have committed to identifying regulations that impede job creation and small business growth. SBE Council looks forward to working with the House Committee on Oversight and Government Reform on solutions and reforms that accelerate job creation, and encourage investment and entrepreneurship.

My name is Karen Kerrigan, President & CEO of SBE Council, a nonpartisan, nonprofit advocacy, research and training organization dedicated to protecting small business and promoting entrepreneurship. With nearly 100,000 members and 250,000 small business activists nationwide, SBE

* These remarks were delivered as testimony given before the Committee on Oversight and Government Reform on February 10, 2011. Karen Kerrigan is President and CEO of Small Business and Entrepreneurship Council.

Council is engaged at the local, state, federal and international levels where we collaborate with elected officials, policy experts and business leaders on initiatives and policies that enhance competitiveness and improve the environment for business start-up and growth.

Currently, business owners remain on edge regarding economic conditions. Uncertainties continue to nag entrepreneurs, and the slow recovery has obviously hampered job creation in the small business sector. A February 4, 2011 report by Gallup's Chief Economist Dennis Jacobe, which analyzed a fourth quarter 2010 Wells Fargo/Gallup Small Business Survey, showed that 42 percent of small business owners hired fewer workers than they needed in 2010. According to the survey, 79 percent remain worried that revenues or sales won't be enough to justify additional employees and 70 percent are concerned about cash flow and their ability to make payroll. In addition, 51 percent are worried about the cost of health care.

While worries about sales and sufficient cash flow remain roadblocks to hiring for small business, government regulation is also a key concern.

In a February 3, 2011 Career Builder survey of 1,350 small businesses, 27 percent of respondents said that government regulation is an impediment to hiring. The cost of health insurance (50 percent) and access to credit (33 percent) were the other chief concerns. (In this survey, 21 percent of small businesses said they plan to hire full-time employees in 2011, up from 20 percent in 2010.)

On top of tough economic conditions, entrepreneurs are truly alarmed by the tidal wave of new federal government regulations that have advanced or been proposed over the past two years. Many business owners are still trying to figure out what the new health care and financial overhaul laws mean for their costs and business operations. Most believe that costs will go up and there will be unintended consequences that impact their firms.

They are concerned about proposed regulations that are in the pipeline at the Department of Labor, Environmental Protection Agency and other agencies, which they believe will impose direct costs on their firms, add to business costs, and constrain private sector investment. Without robust investment by private sector businesses, revenues and sales are hurt. Such is the interdependency of our economy, and small businesses are often damaged the most by the unintended consequences of regulation.

America's small business owners are disproportionately impacted by regulation. The U.S. Small Business Administration's Office of Advocacy has reported that the per-employee cost of federal regulation has reached staggering levels. Their most recent regulatory impact study found that in

2008, the per-employee regulatory cost for small businesses with fewer than 20 employees was $10,585 compared to $7,755 for firms with more than 500 employees.

Regulation of big business also impacts small firms. The threat of new regulation spawns uncertainty for larger enterprises too, leading to a pull back in investment, which not only hurts innovation and job growth but the amount of business that is conducted with entrepreneurs. The findings of a Business Roundtable report —"Mutual Benefits, Shared Growth: Small and Large Companies Working Together," demonstrate the close economic ties between small and large businesses. U.S.-parent operations of the typical U.S. multinational buys goods and services from more than 6,000 American small businesses; buys a total of more than $3 billion in inputs from these small-business suppliers; and relies on these small-business suppliers for more than 24 percent of its total input purchases, according to the report. In sum, small businesses are critically important partners with large multinationals. Regulations that impose requirements, mandates and new costs on big business, affect the bottom-line health of small businesses as suppliers *and* consumers.

As Committee members are aware, state and local governments superimpose an array of regulations over and above those that exist at the federal level. The states vary widely in terms of regulatory scope and costs imposed. For example, a September 2009 analysis —Cost of State Regulations on California Small Business Study|| conducted by Varshney and Associates in conjunction with the California State University of Sacramento College of Business Administration, found the total cost of regulation to be $492.994 billion for the state. So, regulation comes from a variety of government entities, and small businesses experience more hardship in dealing with the cumulative impact.

Mounting regulatory costs from all levels of government are taking their toll on small businesses. With access to capital and credit still tight, along with higher energy and health coverage costs in the picture, small business owners either remain skittish about hiring or lack the resources they need to do so. Of course, this is against the backdrop of a fragile economic recovery. The prospect of additional regulatory burdens and costs drive greater uncertainty. Job creation does not flourish in such an environment.

That is why SBE Council is encouraged about President Obama‘s new regulatory reform strategy. We hope this initiative leads to meaningful relief for small businesses, and the spirit of this effort carries over to regulations currently in the pipeline, and those that will be proposed as part of the new health care and financial overhaul laws. The President‘s directive includes several steps to re-engage and strengthen the voice of small business in the rule making process, including a reminder to government agencies about their existing obligation to small business when new regulations are proposed. We look forward to working with the White House on ways to go about streamlining the regulatory process, identifying outmoded or duplicative regulations, improving the effectiveness of regulations, and lessening burden on small business.

Of course, the small business community was pleased to see the recent moves by OSHA to reexamine its Proposed Interpretation Regarding Noise Exposure and its record-keeping rule on work-related musculoskeletal disorders so it can receive additional input from small business. This just goes to show that when the White House puts a spotlight on the regulatory process, and acknowledges that regulations impact the economy and job growth, such leadership can make a difference.

Areas of Concern

The weak economy has restrained hiring in the small business sector. The collective effect of regulatory activity across the federal government has also curbed confidence and business owner outlook. Hopefully, President Obama‘s new regulatory strategy along with oversight by Congress will improve the policy environment. However, key areas of regulatory activity will continue to cause uncertainty for small business owners. Proposed regulations in the pipeline will have a direct cost impact on their firms. In addition, small businesses that are dependent upon the vigor of specific industries like the energy sector, for example share deep concerns about their survivability due to regulatory activity not favorable to energy production and investment in the United States.

Energy and the EPA

The general regulatory thrust of the Administration with regard to the treatment of our traditional and predominant energy sources will lead to less energy, higher energy prices, the disincentive to manufacture in the U.S., and job loss. Caps and restrictions are being imposed on how much America can use and produce, which will drive costs higher. Unfortunately, small businesses and their workforce will bear the brunt of higher costs and job loss if certain initiatives at the Environmental Protection Agency (EPA) move forward.

From EPA‘s set of rules on electric power generators to greenhouse gas (GHG) regulation, to its reconsideration of the National Ambient Air Quality Standards for Ground-Level Ozone to ―Boiler MACT‖ industrial emission standards, this one agency alone has the potential to undermine the economic recovery while putting our businesses at a competitive disadvantage in the global marketplace. Energy drives business and the economy it all starts with energy. Higher prices for all forms of energy will mean less capital for jobs and investment. If it costs more to make things here in the U.S., investment and jobs will continue to move overseas.

Energy Development and Production: The U.S. has been blessed with abundant natural resources to support our growing energy needs. Unfortunately, the oil and natural gas sector is getting mixed signals from the federal government in regard to the future of offshore drilling and development in general. More than 4 million jobs in small businesses are supported by the oil and natural gas industry, according to the American Petroleum Institute (API) but new restrictions and general uncertainty threaten these businesses and their workforce. Conversely, hundreds of thousands of new jobs can be created if the federal government develops a more rational and stable policy toward domestic energy development.

PATIENT PROTECTION AND AFFORDABLE CARE ACT (PPACA)

During the debate over PPACA, the new health care law was portrayed as an effort to reduce health coverage costs. But the early outcomes of its implementation show rising premiums, confusion over the grandfather rule, unknowns regarding what type of plans will be available once regulations fully take effect, and serious concern about the employer mandate. New compliance mandates (expanded 1099 and health premium reporting) will drive costs higher, and there is fear that new regulations will curtail the availability of what have been affordable choices in the marketplace.

SBE Council did not support PPACA‘s passage. We have long advocated an approach that encourages competition, leads to more affordable prices and expands upon what is working in the marketplace (like Health Savings Accounts). Business owners' concerns about the resources they will need to expend to comply with the law, along with their view that health coverage costs will continue to increase under PPACA (as a result of tax increases and additional regulation), add to their general uncertainty about labor costs moving forward. PPACA also establishes a threshold for when the employer mandate kicks in, which may have the effect of retarding job growth.

FEDERAL GOVERNMENT PROCUREMENT

Recent actions and proposals by the Obama Administration have the potential to set small business owners back in their efforts to bid on and access government contracts. For small businesses that currently operate successfully in the federal government marketplace, the following new rules and proposed initiatives will undercut their ability to compete, which will lead to job loss in these firms.

Project Labor Agreements (PLAs): In April 2010, President Obama finalized Executive Order 13502, which encourages and authorizes the use of union-only PLAs on federal construction projects. Union-only PLAs restrict competition by requiring that a contract be awarded only to companies who agree to collective bargaining and union hiring. Most small to mid-size firms can't compete under such a scenario. Federal government procurement rules require a competitive bidding process, and PLAs run counter to the rules of fairness, transparency and best value for taxpayers.

"High Road Initiative": The Obama Administration has been working on an initiative that would grant competitive advantage to government contractors whose salaries and benefits meet wage and benefit standards established by the federal government. Such standards could be higher than the norm offered by small businesses, which would put small contractors at a competitive disadvantage in the federal procurement space. Taxpayer costs may also escalate. Small business stakeholders have had little input into the initiative, but they need to if the Administration moves forward as it will have an impact on the jobs that small government contractors provide.

3 Percent Withholding Mandate: The mandate, advanced as part of Section 511 of the Tax Increase Prevention and Reconciliation Act of 2005 (P.L. 109-222), will increase government costs and bureaucracy at all levels (local, state and federal); raise costs for taxpayers; and restrict cash flow for small firms. If not repealed, small contractors will find it more difficult to compete for contracts, which threaten jobs in this sector.

THE FEDERAL GOVERNMENT AND AMERICA'S WORKPLACES

Plan/Prevent/Protect: The U.S. Department of Labor (DoL) asserts it does not have enough resources to ensure that businesses are complying with all federal workplace regulations. Therefore, they are embarking on a "Plan/Prevent/Protect" regulatory initiative which, according to their words, —Employers and others must ‗find and fix' violations that is, assure compliance before a Labor Department investigator arrives at the workplace.|| The new regulatory program will require businesses and other regulated entities to develop extensive, time-consuming plans and internal processes with their employees that will serve as a —check|| for DoL on how and whether businesses are complying with the law.

The initiative involves several agencies under DoL's auspices including the Wage and Hour Division (WHD), the Occupational Safety and Health Administration (OSHA), the Office of Federal Contract Compliance Programs, the Mine Safety and Health Administration, and the Employee Benefits Security Administration. Each agency will propose rules that require businesses to develop programs to comply with the law, and submit them to DoL enforcement agencies. For example, as part of —Plan/Protect/Prevent|| WHD is expected to propose a requirement that employers provide workers with information about how their pay is calculated, how they develop job classifications, document the job classifications (identifying who is —exempt|| or an independent contractor and why), and hold training sessions to make sure everyone understands the differences in these classifications. For small businesses, the totality of the agency-wide Plan/Protect/Prevent program would be a significant burden if not a nightmare.

Shift at DoL: A robust change has been underway at DoL. The Wage and Hour Division (WHD) budget has been increased to hire 288 new inspectors (which has already grown from 731 inspectors in 2009, to 894 in Q1 in 2010). Other budget features include the addition of 130 safety and health inspectors, 25 whistle-blowers, and 20 full-time employees to —restore|| OSHA's rule-making capabilities. Certainly, we want the DoL to have the staff and resources it needs to do its job, but we are concerned that the department will move further away from constructive engagement and helping businesses comply with the law toward encouraging employees to file complaints and grievances.

"Bridge to Justice": The DoL has recently implemented a new partnership with the American Bar Association (ABA) that will refer workers who call to report (or ask questions about) alleged wage and hour violations, or those involving the Family and Medical Leave Act (FMLA), to ABA-sanctioned lawyers. A toll-free number will be provided to individuals, which will connect them to a network of lawyers. The WHD says it does not have the staff resources to review all the incoming complaints, so it has called on the ABA for assistance. Small business owners are very concerned about this new hotline-to-a-lawyer program in that it may very well amount to a feeder system for legal action against business. Dealing with such inquiries by a lawyer will be time consuming and expensive, particularly if a small business owner is forced to hire legal representation. High legal costs can break a small firm. No doubt many small business owners will settle these claims (even if innocent).

Dodd-Frank Financial Overhaul Legislation

New regulations being proposed (and to be proposed) under the auspices of Dodd-Frank have the potential to further restrict access to, and raise the cost of, capital and credit for small business owners. Proposed Federal Reserve rules regarding interchange fees and forthcoming Consumer Financial Protection Bureau (CFPB) regulations, for example, could make a currently challenging problem much worse for small business owners. Without access to capital and credit, or if costs increase, small businesses will remain reluctant to expand their firms and hire. Small business owners remain unsure as what the financial overhaul law will mean to their firms, although they are beginning to see new monthly fees on bank checking accounts and are being told that changes will occur in the cost and availability of financial services they currently use. Such uncertainty adds to the general sense that it remains a risky time to hire.

CONCLUSION

As noted previously in my testimony, SBE Council is pleased that the Administration will conduct a comprehensive review of federal regulations.

We are pleased that the Committee is hosting this hearing today to shed light on burdensome regulation and its effect on job creation and healthy economic growth. With Congress and the White House both focused on this important issue, SBE Council is hopeful that the efforts will lead to common ground -- particularly on reforms that will place a check on federal regulators, and institutionalize measures that require agencies to more carefully review the cost and impact of their actions on the economy, small businesses and job creation.

Chairman Issa and Ranking Member Cummings, SBE Council appreciates the opportunity to provide input to the Committee. We look forward to providing solutions that will help small businesses create jobs and move our economy back to strong levels of growth. Thank you for your leadership.

Karen Kerrigan

Bio

Karen Kerrigan is one of the world's leading experts on policies, training initiatives and programs that benefit entrepreneurs. She is widely known for developing collaborative relationships with business associations, public policy groups, media, government, advocacy organizations, universities, educational foundations and the private sector that have led to substantive reforms and initiatives to help encourage and sustain entrepreneurship across the globe. Ms. Kerrigan is President & CEO of the *Small Business & Entrepreneurship Council,* a prominent and respected advocacy and research organization. She is Founder of *Women Entrepreneurs Inc.,* an organization dedicated to helping women business owners succeed through education, networking and advocacy.

Ms. Kerrigan travels across the U.S. and the globe conducting training seminars on starting and growing businesses; helping business associations build their capacity; and working with government officials at the highest levels to develop and implement policies and programs to encourage and sustain entrepreneurial activity. She co-hosts the highly acclaimed *Growth Without Barriers* webcast series – an interactive training and educational broadcast that reaches hundreds of thousands of small business owners each year.

Ms. Kerrigan regularly testifies before the U.S. Congress on issues that impact America's small business and entrepreneurial sector. She is frequently called on to advise the White House, and leaders in government agencies about recommendations and strategies to help small businesses and encourage their growth. Working with the U.S. State Department, she meets regularly with global delegations visiting the U.S. who wish to learn about public policy recommendations and Best Practices in entrepreneurial training that will enhance and sustain business start- up and growth. In June 2002 she was appointed to serve on the *National Women's Business Council.* In September 2002 she was appointed by the U.S. Treasury Secretary to serve on the Taxpayer Advocacy Panel (TAP). In 2003, at the President's Economic Summit in Waco, TX she led the Small Business session, the outcome being the enactment of key legislative and policy ideas identified at the event. She also participated in the December 2004 White House Economic Summit where she served as a speaker on the Affordable Health Care panel.

She helped construct the Women Entrepreneurship in the 21st Century conferences sponsored by the U.S. Department of Labor (DoL) and Small Business Administration, and organized the National Women's Leadership Summit (Oct. 2004) and *Flex Options for Women* with the DoL's Women's Bureau. In May 2005, WE Inc. co-sponsored the first MidEast/North Africa Women's Business Summit in Tunis, Tunisia where Kerrigan also led a delegation of U.S. businesswomen to the groundbreaking event. In July 2005, she was appointed as a member of the National Advisory Committee for Labor Provisions of U.S. Free Trade Agreements to represent the business community. In November 2007, she was appointed to the board of directors of the *Center for International Private Enterprise.* She serves on the U.S.-Iraq Business Dialog and is an advisory board member of the *National Association of Women Business Owners (NAWBO), Moms in Business, Enterprising Women magazine,* Verizon's Consumer Advisory Board and the Economic

Advisory Committee of *Broadband for America.* She is a founding member of the *World Entrepreneurship Forum.* In February 2010, she agreed to join the Bipartisan Debt Reduction Task Force, co-chaired by former Senator Pete Domenici and former OMB Director Dr. Alice Rivlin.

In the February 2006 issue of *Inc. Magazine*, Kerrigan was listed on the "Best Friends in D.C." list for small business owners, profiled as a *"power broker and activist"* with "serious clout" for entrepreneurs. In May 2005 *The Hill* newspaper called Kerrigan "the hardest working woman in show business" and credited her leadership of the SBE Council for making it one of the top 5 influential groups representing small business. *Fortune Small Business* named Ms. Kerrigan to its Power 30 list of key advocates in Washington in September 2000. In 1995, *National Journal* named Ms. Kerrigan to its short list of "K Street" activists most likely to have an impact on Capitol Hill. *Campaigns and Elections Magazine* named her as one of its "Rising Stars in Politics" in its April 1996 issue. In November 2009, she was presented with the "Small Business Advocate of the Year" award by the New York Enterprise Report.

Her commentary, analysis and written work have appeared in many of the nation's leading newspapers. For more than a decade she wrote a regular column for the *American City Business Journals* - an influential network of weekly business newspapers in 50 major markets. She has appeared on *ABC`s Nightline*, The McLaughlin Group, *CNN*, *CNBC,* and *Fox News, Fox Business* among others. She has been a guest on hundreds of radio talk shows.

Ms. Kerrigan is a native of New York, and holds a BA degree in Political Science from Cortland College (SUNY). She resides in Northern Virginia.

INDEX

V

W